Hybrid Intrusion Detection System

Hybrid Intrusion Detection System

Dr. Asma Shaikh

NAMYA PRESS.com

Published by

Namya Press

India: 213, Vardan House, 7/28 Ansari Road Darya Ganj - Delhi India 110002
USA: 10685-B Hazelhurst Dr. # 31013 Houston, Texas USA - 77043
Email: namyapress@gmail.com
Website: https://namyapress.com

Edition	:	First Published in 2023 (Namya Press)
Title	:	Hybrid Intrusion Detection System
Author	:	Dr. Asma Shaikh
ISBN	:	978-93-5545-537-6
Copyright	:	© Dr. Asma Shaikh. 2023 All Rights Reserved

Abstract

There is a notable rise in the demand for data security as systems administration applications continue to evolve and integrate software-based frameworks. More and more sophisticated Internet attacks can pass standard firewall and antivirus defense. To help make the network safer, extra protection is also necessary. An intrusion detection system might be used as an extra layer of defence technology (IDS). Signature-based detection and anomaly-based detection are two methods of intrusion detection that are employed. An anomaly-based system is used to detect anomalous behaviour. Signature-based IDS employs rules to detect intrusions. Signature-based IDS scans signatures for attacks, however it is unable to detect unknown threats but provider less false alarms. Anomaly-based IDS, on the other hand, may detect unknown attacks due to its enhanced examination of normal behaviour but produce more false alarms. The essential factor for a network management to choose an IDS is the trade-off between the ability to identify new types of attacks and the ability to produce lesser false alarms.

The proposed and implemented intelligent intrusion detection system in this dissertation will combine the advantage of Signature based detection and Anomaly-based detection techniques. This book proposes a novel intrusion detection system that includes Signature-based detection engine and Anomaly based detection engine. Signature based Detection Engine is used for checking the attacks from the Signature Ruleset using Decision Tree. It receives accuracy of 96%. Whereas, Anomaly Based Detection Engine uses Deep learning algorithms to detect anomalies in the networks and receives an accuracy of 97.25%. The combination of both detection system gives the accuracy of 98.98% for detection of intrusion. The major advantage of proposed IDS is capable of detecting a broad variety of attacks with a high detection rate and a low false alarm rate. The proposed system was trained and tested on three popular datasets, Network Security Laboratory Knowledge Discovery in Databases (NSL-KDD), UNSW Canberra's (UNSW2015), the Canadian Institute for Cybersecurity

2017 (CICIDS2017) datasets. The effectiveness of proposed Intelligent IDS model was validated using the following measures, namely precision, accuracy, F-measure, recall. In this book, Computational complexity is measured with Big O notations, significant number of floating-point operations (FLOPs), the number of multiply-accumulate (MAC) operations and number of binary operations (BOP).

Contents

List of Acronyms and Abbreviations

AE	:	AutoEncoder
ANN	:	Artificial Neural Network
AIDS	:	Anomaly Based Intrusion Detection system
CIA	:	Confidentiality Integrity Availability
CIC	:	Canadian Institute for Cybersecurity
CNN	:	Convolutional Neural Network
DBN	:	Deep Belief Network
DoS	:	Denial of Service
DDoS	:	Distributed Denial of Service
DT	:	Decision Tree
FN	:	False Negative
FP	:	False Positive
FPR	:	False Positive Rate
HIDS	:	Host-based Intrusion Detection System
HTTP	:	Hypertext Transfer Protocol
ICMP	:	Internet Control Message Protocol
IDS	:	Intrusion Detection System
IP	:	Internet Protocol
IPS	:	Intrusion Prevention System
ISO	:	International Organization for Standardization
KDD	:	Knowledge Discovery and Data mining
KNN	:	K-Nearest Neighbors
LAN	:	Local Area Network
NIDS	:	Network Intrusion Detection System
ReLU	:	Rectifier Linear Unit
RNN	:	Reccurent Neural Network
ROC	:	Receiver Operating Characteristic
SIDS	:	Signature based Intrusion Detection System
SMOTE	:	Synthetic Minority Over-sampling Technique
SOM	:	Self-Organizing Map

SVM	:	Support Vector Machine
TCP	:	Transmission Control Protocol
TN	:	True Negative
TP	:	True Positive
TPR	:	True Positive Rate
U2R	:	User To Root
UDP	:	User Datagram Protocol
VLAN	:	Virtual Local Area Network
VM	:	Virtual Machine

1

Introduction

1.1 Overview

Nowadays, all organisations and devices are internet-linked[1]. Internet-based devices are more sensitive to attacks. Over time, Internet-based attacks have become more advanced, to the degree that they can bypass basic security measures such as antivirus scanners and firewalls[2]. The fast growth in systems administration applications and software-based frameworks make it imperative to develop stronger security measures for fighting against digital threats. Identification, detection and avoidance of attacks in the connected world of computing has assumed prominence. According to Cisco's Annual Internet Report (2018-2023) [3], an average person would have 3.6 networked devices connected in 2023 which will increase from 2.4 in 2018. This will result in a total networked device population of 29.3 billion. Additionally, the report outlines show attacks increased by 776 percent between 100 Gbps and 400 Gbps between 2018 and 2019 respectively and will continue to expand in the coming years.

A possible method of enhancing network security is to include an additional layer that protects the network structure, which can be done through an Intrusion detection system (IDS). An Intrusion detection system (IDS) is a software application that monitors and reports on attacks on a device or network. They are in responsible of spotting anomalies that threaten the integrity, confidentiality, and accessibility of system resources. In addition to determining attacks through ongoing network monitoring and determining the range and depth of IDS is essential for ensuring network security since it detects intrusions.

The deployment model and the detection model are the two categories into which intrusion detection may be divided. The deployment mechanism can either be host-based or network-based. Software that monitors and detects network traffic before it enters the network is known as network-based IDS. Simultaneously, host-based intrusion detection and prevention (IDP) tools are placed on the server to monitor and identify unusual activity.

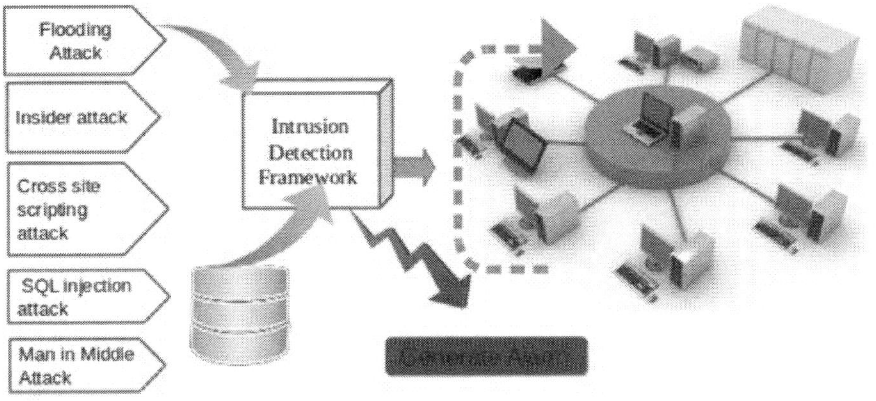

Figure 1.1: General Architecture of IDS

The detection model encompasses signature-based and anomaly-based intrusion detection systems. Signature-based IDS scans the ruleset for specific patterns or signatures and provides warnings if they are detected. Without a signature in the ruleset, the security breach[4] will go unnoticed, but an anomaly-based IDS would identify behaviour that is out of pattern for the user. Anomaly-based intrusion detection systems (IDS) are used to identify unknown threats. The anomalous behaviour is identified. The detection of abnormalities provides context for the network's expected performance[5].

General architecture of IDS is given in Figure 1.1. The Figure depicts different attacks like flooding attack, insider attack, cross site scripting attack, SQL injection attack and Man in Middle attack . IDS is capable of detecting these attacks and generate alarm on detection, eventually protecting the network. IDS does it by detecting any substantial changes in the performance of network as it attempts to identify malicious traffic by detecting deviations from well-known regular traffic patterns. Despite this, due to increase in the number of new attacks and their complexity, existing IDS fall short of identifying novel and undiscovered threats.

1.2 Major Challenges

- Increased network traffic: Recent demands and improvements in information technology applications have increased network traffic between hosts to unprecedented levels. The network-based IDS must be capable of handling continuous processing and a high load.
- IDS must continuously keep track of the network for any intrusions, identify and prevent attacks by applying policies, and determine the kind of intrusions and penetration level.
- When anomaly-based or signature-based IDS techniques are used separately the main concern is the high rate of false-positive alerts and low detection rate of novel attacks.
- Problem of Imbalanced classifications, which is classification built with the assumption that each class had an equally large sample size. Models with low prediction accuracy, especially for minorities, are the outcome of this. Typically, the minority class has a greater impact on the issue, which makes it more vulnerable to categorization mistakes for the minority class than for the majority class.
- Feature selection is useful in eliminating unnecessary and redundant data, increasing learning accuracy, and improving result comprehension. It is very important part of preprocessing in Machine learning algorithms. Dimensionality reduction in terms of efficiency and efficacy, several current approaches for feature selection and feature extraction are being challenged by the recent rise in the attack surface. The total number of potential security risk exposures makes up the attack surface. It can also be defined as the sum of all existing, potential, and known controls across all network. Extraction of essential features is difficult due to different types of features and different nature .
- IDS in use employ either anomaly- or signature-based detection techniques. Building an IDS is challenging because of the complexity of the design.
- Existing IDS are "signature-based or rule based" because they look for a specific signature pattern and a specified pattern. These patterns make up the ruleset used by the IDS. Each packet is compared to a stored signature to identify infiltration. This IDS will identify an intrusion using a signature. Signature-based IDS identifies attacks based on signatures, but it cannot

identify unknown attacks since it doesn't analyse variations in behaviour.

- Anomaly-based IDS is commonly used to identify attacks because of deviations in the typical behaviour of malicious attackers from normal behaviour. In addition, because anomaly-based IDS doesn't require signatures to be previously saved, it may identify unknown threats but generate more false alarm.
- The quality of an IDS's signature ruleset is directly proportional to the strength of the IDS itself. As long as it isn't regularly updated, it won't be able to keep up with the most recent threats and will not notify you of them. Additionally, your systems are susceptible until a new threat is added to the signature ruleset, so the current attacks remain a major risk.
- Some system combines this approaches, but none of them have adapted deep learning with updating signature into the rule set

1.3 Research Questions

Following the discussion of developing an intrusion detection system, the dissertation investigates and answers several research issues.

The following are the questions:

- How to utilise the Signature-based detection technique to identify known attacks using existing signatures stored in ruleset?
- How to implement novel Anomaly-based detection technique for detecting unknown attacks, in case Signature based detection technique fails to do so?
- Is it possible to combine signature and anomaly-based detection techniques for effective detection of known and unknown attacks
- How successful is this new technique when compared to conventional IDS?

1.4 Problem Definition

The internet and computer networks have been a primary security focus in the present threat environment. Cyberspace security is a collection of technologies and practises aimed to safeguard computers, networks, software, and data files from attack, unauthorised access, modification, or destruction. An intrusion detection system's functional concept is to detect an intrusion as it occurs. However, it is very difficult since the majority of IDS suffer from false alarms [6]. Signature-based intrusion detection systems are particularly quick and accurate since they identify known intrusions by comparing incoming traffic with signature databases [7]. Signature-based intrusion detection systems have become outdated due to their inability to identify new threats if signatures are not updated [8]. Another problem with signature-based IDS is that the database contains a huge number of signatures that are compared to arriving and departing packets. Because this approach takes longer to identify a malicious packet, it has a negative impact on network security. Anomaly-based intrusion detection systems, on the other hand, records the host's typical behaviour, and any variation from that behaviour is recognised as an intrusion. Anomaly-based intrusion detection systems are very effective in detecting new threats. Because there is so much data in today's network environments, the normal profile evolves with time. IDS are constructed using either signature-based or anomaly-based detection methods. They are highly diverse in design and rarely integrated with existent IDS. The proposed system must be designed to create an intrusion detection system (IDS) by combining the features of a Signature-based intrusion detection system (SIDS) with low false-positive rates and Anomaly-based Intrusion detection systems (AIDS) with the ability to identify unknown attacks[9]. It will help in the detection of unknown attacks and reduces the probability of false alarms. In a nutshell, this idea aims to solve the problem of reducing false alarm rate and detecting unknown attacks by integrating Signature and Anomaly based Intrusion Detection techniques.

1.5 Research Statement

It is critical to examine the existing protection methods and related processes to identify hidden attacks because of new security problems with intrusion detection notifications generated by systems. The process involves developing new security methods, implementing a hybrid approach to increase performance, ensuring the network's security, and notifying network administrators of a potential threat. Combining signature based and anomaly based approach helps to detect unknown attacks and reduce false positive rates of notification of intrusion. Further using deep learning algorithms, the presented enriched data representation and framework allows the development of precise, effective, and intelligent intrusion detection systems for Networks.

The above mentioned notion leads to the following book statement

Design and Development of Intrusion Detection System for Improved Performance by Combining Signature and Anomaly-based Approaches.

1.6 Objective of Research

The objective of the research work is given below:

- **Objective 1:** Designing of new methodology for signature based intrusion detection system using decision tree.
- **Objective 2:** Designing of new methodology for anomaly based intrusion detection using deep learning model - CNN with ResNet50.
- **Objective 3:** Designing and implementation of an intelligent intrusion detection system by combining Signature and Anomaly based Intrusion Detection, capable of detecting a broad variety of attacks with a high detection rate and a low false alarm rate.

1.7 Research Methodology

A review of more than 110 articles was done as part of the research approach. The papers covered a variety of subjects. The subjects discussed included anomalies, signatures, existing intrusion detection system, algorithms.

The methods employed to conduct this research include:

1. Conduct a search for threats, attack detection based on anomalies, attack detection based on signature and hybrid models.
2. Develop a set of predefined database signatures and Signature based detection module to detect attack from predefined signatures.
3. If attacks are not detected by the Signature based IDS then go the next module to classify it using an anomaly-based detection technique.
4. Combined both the module into the system and detect false positive and false negative data, calculate the outcome of the test data to measure the performance for the proposed solution.
5. Compare results with other available IDS using evaluation parameter metrics.

1.8 Overview of Research Tasks

The following tasks are performed in this effort to address the specified research:

- **Conduct Literature Search** i. Conduct a literature search on current intrusion detection techniques and attacks, emphasising intrusion detection system approaches. Because there are two types of intrusion detection systems, the literature search will include explanations and procedures for each. ii. Conduct a review of the articles on this issue gathered and describe the conclusions and findings.

- **Design and Develop** i. A novel technique for signature-based analysis utilising predefined signature ruleset; ii. A novel technique for the anomaly-based intrusion detection system.
- **Create a Detection Model that is a combination of the previous two.** i. Propose detection approaches that incorporate both types of attack detection methods into a single model. This is done to identify any kind of attack known as well as unknown attack. ii. Create signatures from anomalies detected.
- **Conduct tests and evaluations** i. Use Google's Tensorflow to create an intrusion detection system. Tensorflow from Google was used to carry out the tests since it allows developers to view the network design. The experiments are carried out in the following setting. RAM: 8GB Intel ® Core TM i5-5200U CPU @ 2.20 GHz CPU: Intel ® Core TM i5-5200 Ubuntu Programming (OS) Numpy, Sci-kit-learn, pandas, and Tensorflow are Python libraries that were used. ii. Using the LibPack library, collect packets from the network. iii. Use a signature-based Rule set to detect attacks with unique signatures. iv. If the Signature-based detection engine fails to identify an attack,then control goes to the Anomaly-based detection engine, which uses the CNN ResNet50 classifier to detect anomalies. v. If attack detected then generate alarm and shows three most probable attacks with percentages.
- **Disseminate Work Results** 1. Write and submit articles to appropriate journals for publication. 2. Also disseminate research work by presenting papers in various international level conferences.

1.9 Contributions of Research

The work described in this book builds on prior IDS research and contributes to the development of the next-generation IDS. The primary contributions of this book are as follows:

- A comprehensive literature review of IDS-related literature over the last decade. The study examines the most commonly used IDS datasets in the literature, as well as the machine learning and deep learning techniques used to construct IDS and the cyber threats that are covered/detected. The study pinpoints the flaws in existing IDS and identifies research needs. An expandable cyber threat taxonomy is offered to better analyse the cyber attacks covered in IDS. Comprehensive literature review have been published in papers[9],[10].

- Designing and developing an intrusion detection system framework for both signature and anomaly detection techniques using Decision tree and CNN ResNet 50 model respectively. The following research work has been published in papers [11],[12].
- Proposal of intelligent Intrusion Detection System capable of detecting well known as well as zero-day attacks with higher accuracy. The model was trained and tested on three popular datasets, Network Security Laboratory Knowledge Discovery in Databases (NSL-KDD), UNSW Canberra's (UNSW2015), the Canadian Institute for Cybersecurity 2017 (CICIDS2017) datasets. The effectiveness of proposed Intelligent IDS model was validated using the following measures, namely precision, accuracy, F-measure, recall. Evaluation results have been published in research paper [13].
- Also an important contribution is the design and implementation of an intelligent system that allows the system to learn from previous intrusion attempts and prepare rules.These research work investigations have been published in research paper [14],[15].

1.10 Organization of book

The book is organized as follows:

- **Chapter 2** outlines key principles in intrusion detection. It explains what a computer attack is, what an intrusion detection system is, and how the area has evolved through time. The pros and limitations of several types of IDSs are discussed. The contributions of machine learning and deep learning to this topic are examined, as well as the many datasets mentioned in this dissertation. The most often used metrics are finally established. Existing work on intrusion detection using machine learning and deep learning methods is presented in this chapter. The various models are described in depth, along with a brief explanation of how they function. The approaches and outcomes are presented in order, then find out of research gaps and issues in existing techniques.
- **Chapter 3** shows proposed system of Intrusion Detection System , implementation of Combined approach of IDS using Signature based IDS and Anomaly Based IDS using decision

tree and CNN ResNet 50 model respectively.

- **Chapter 4** presents Signature based Intrusion Detection System, their advantages and disadvantages. Implementation of SIDS using decision tree, how to form decision tree is also given. Also shown here creation of rules for Signature based IDS using SNORT rules and mapping of Rules with NSL KDD dataset features. Also shown result received when created SIDS Module.
- **Chapter 5** describes Anomaly based Intrusion Detection System, their advantages and disadvantages. Implementation of AIDS using Convolutional Neural Network using LeeNet5 and ResNet50. Also given algorithm of ResNet50. Also shown here three different datasets and implemented ResNet50 on datasets like NSL- KDD dataset, UNSW15 Dataset and CICIDS2017 dataset. As steps it shows, features extracted from different Datasets. Also shown result received when created AIDS Module.
- **Chapter 6** examines implementation and performance evaluation is given . Results of each phase is given with evaluation parameters like accuracy, precision, recall and F1 score.
- **Chapter 7** is conclusion chapter with a summary of the dissertation's key topics.The importance of proposed intrusion detection is emphasised, as well as future development.

2

Literature Survey

This chapter delves into the context of the literature searches and summarises the results of the literature review. Due to the degree of information necessary for this book, extensive literature review was conducted. The following sections explain different techniques for intrusion detection first. Following that, a section on related literature on signature-based or misuse based and anomaly-based intrusion detection is provided. This section discusses current IDS publications, analysing both research trends and shortfalls. This research outlines the primary methods and datasets utilised, and finishes with a discussion of the merits and shortcomings of modern IDS. To do this, Google Scholar and IEEE Xplore searches were conducted using the terms "*Intrusion Detection System*" OR "*IDS*" with results further filtered to include works published between 1998 and 2022. A review of more than 110 articles was done as part of the research approach.

2.1 Overview

Network security is described as the "protection of networks, data, and systems in network" [10]. Intrusion detection is a technique for detecting malicious activity directed at computer and networking systems. An IDS monitors network traffic in order to detect potentially hazardous events. A device or network's Intrusion Detection System (IDS) detects and reports threats [11]. They are in charge of identifying abnormalities that impact the system's confidentiality, availability, and integrity. In addition to detecting attacks, an IDS performs active network monitoring and evaluation of the comprehensiveness of the intrusion. The following category, as illustrated in Figure 1, may be used to study intrusion detection model. Many experiments have been carried out to protect information systems from unwanted intrusion. Despite this, more study is required to ensure the long-term viability of network-based information systems (both wired and wireless). Advances in network communication technologies are linked to increased network activity and the growth of network attacks such as Denial of Service (DoS) attacks, worms, virus exploits, and other types of attacks. For this reason, network operators and managers must shoulder challenging responsibilities to keep the Internet accessible. In today's computing world, implementing adequate security measures to guard against computer and network breaches has become a vital concern. Furthermore, the number of network-based computer services has risen substantially, as has the number of programmes operating on networked computers[12]. An intrusion detection system (IDS) is a computer or network monitoring tool that detects unauthorised or unusual activity in a company's computer system or network. A network of sensors or hosts scattered across the network make an IDS. This system has the ability to monitor network traffic, gather it locally, and then report the data to a management console. Network-based intrusion detection uses signature-based and anomaly-based methods. The goal of efficient SIDS detection is to accurately identify previously identified intrusion based on patterns found in data. While the rule-based method is based on rules that recognize current intrusions, it does not create many false alarms due to the rules knowing intrusion. Analyzing and reporting abnormal computational behavioural patterns is part of anomaly detection. Concerning anomaly-based detection, models of expected system behaviour can be constructed from the observed data and differentiate between significant deviations and exceptions. To detect anomalies, one must look for a typical behaviour that does not fit the norm. the anomaly detection technique can assess new or undetected intrusions Organisations are increasingly seeking solutions to these problems to protect their brand. Installing an intrusion detection system is a more secure option (IDS). Because these systems now rely on signatures of the attacks used to identify an intruder or changes in the System's behavioural patterns. Types of IDS are shown in Figure 2.1 , here IDS is categorize as per deployment based and detection based. Deployment based IDSs are Host based IDS or Network based IDS. Detection based IDSs are Anomaly based or Signature based IDS.

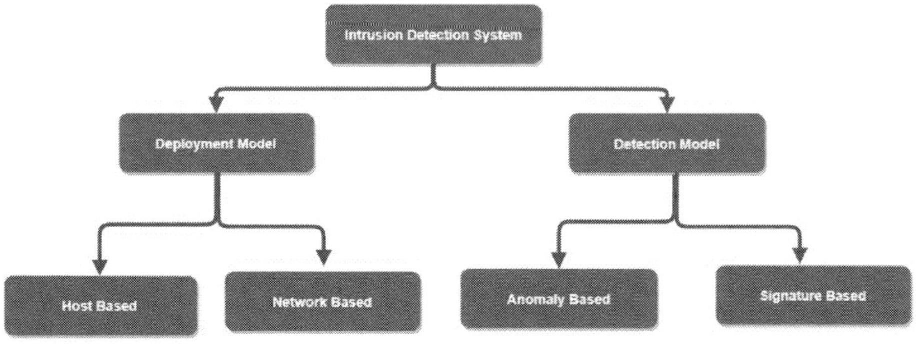

Figure 2.1: Types of IDS

2.2 Information Security

Network is used to pass information from one system to another system. Information security is defined as ”actions taken to prevent unauthorised use, abuse, modification, or denial of use of knowledge facts, data, or information”[13] . Information security is defined using C-I-A triad is shown Figure 2.2. The ISO 27000 International Standard [14] defines confidentiality, non-repudiation, and integrity as follows:

- **Confidentiality:** The property of keeping information secret, rendering it unavailable to unauthorised persons, or releasing it to unauthorised entities.
- **Integrity:** The attributes of integrity include accuracy and completeness.
- **Ease of access:** Access to and usage of information on demand is provided by approved entities.
- **Accuracy/Authenticity:** The capacity of an entity to be an accurate representation of itself.
- **Non-denial:** The capacity to demonstrate that a stated event or action took place, as well as the parties that took part.

Auditability is a system's ability to monitor all actions made by humans or computers within the system in a permanent, non-bypassable way (user-involvement).

Despite having outlined the aims of information security, companies and consumers remain susceptible to a significant number of breaches and attack in the actual world. Employee-driven causes (such as mistakes and ignorance) are origins of a data breach, however, these variables are outside the scope of this research and will not be included.

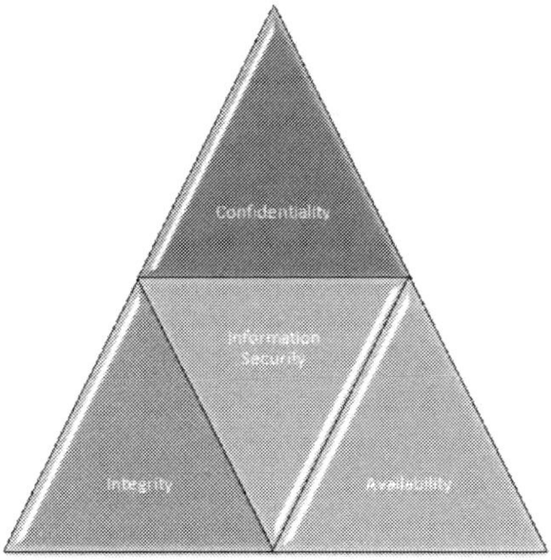

Figure 2.2: Information security

2.3 Taxonomy of Threats

A cyberattack is deemed active if it modifies or affects any part of a network or system. For instance, it may impair performance or corrupt data. Even the Cloud environment is subjected to some of these security concerns[9]. Kendall [16] established one of the first categories of attacks. They classed intrusions as DoS, R2L, U2R, and Probing.

1. Backdoor Trojan

A backdoor Trojan infects the victim's system with a backdoor vulnerability, enabling the attacker to obtain remote, and almost entire, control. The Trojan is often used to connect a number of victims' computers to form a botnet or zombie network, but attackers may also use it for other types of criminality.

2. Attack using cross-site scripting (XSS)

XSS attacks[113] inject malicious code into a legitimate website or application script in order to get a user's personal information, often via the use of third-party online resources. Although attackers commonly utilise JavaScript for XSS assaults, they may also use Microsoft VCScript, ActiveX, or Adobe Flash.

3. Denial-of-service (DoS) and Distributed denial-of-service (DDoS)

Denial-of-service (DoS) [9] and Distributed denial-of-service (DDoS) assaults overload a system's resources, preventing it from responding to service requests, hence impairing the system's capacity to function. Frequently, this strike serves as a prelude to a subsequent onslaught.

4. Tunneling of the DNS

Cybercriminals utilise DNS tunnelling, a transactions protocol, to exchange application data, such as discreetly extracting data or establishing a communication channel with an unknown server for purposes such as command and control (C&C) exchanges.

5. Malware

Malware [9] is a kind of malicious software that may disable afflicted computers. The majority of malware versions destroy data by destroying or erasing files that are required for the operating system to function properly.

6. Phishing

Phishing schemes are designed to steal consumers' login passwords or other sensitive information, such as credit card numbers. In this situation, fraudsters send victims emails or text messages that seem to come from a credible source, complete with bogus URLs.

7. Ransomware

Ransomware is sophisticated software that exploits system vulnerabilities and uses powerful encryption to encrypt data or system functions. Cybercriminals employ ransomware to extort money in return for the system's release. The addition of extortion methods to ransomware is a recent development.

8. SQL injection attacks

Additional SQL injection [9] information is available in the 2021 Threat Index. SQL injection attacks insert malicious code into susceptible applications, displaying the results of backend database queries and executing instructions or similar operations that the user did not request.

9. Zero-day vulnerability

Zero-day exploits take use of previously undisclosed hardware and software vulnerabilities. These problems may remain for days, months, or even years before engineers become aware of them.

10. Probing

This attack is used to observe and conduct surveillance on a distant target, such as port scanning, in order to gather information, "duration of connection" and "source bytes" are the most important aspects.

11. U2R

To get root/administrator capabilities in the victim, an attacker exploits a vulnerability by logging into the victim's system using a regular user account and e.g. buffer overflow assaults. This sort of attack is also called a "unauthorised access to local super user (root) privileges attack." The "number of files created" and the "number of shell prompts executed" are both relevant aspects. The attacker acquires local access to the target workstation by guessing the victim's password via illegal access from a distant computer.

12. R2L

Features to consider: A host's "number of unsuccessful login attempts" and "duration of connection" are both network-level properties.

2.4 Types of IDS

IDSs are classified into two categories according to the deployment methods.

2.4.1 Host-based IDS

A Host-based IDS (HIDS) is intended for a particular computer system and lives in an individual computer system. Primary server system named host (host) is most commonly installed to monitor the actions of just the server systems[10]. Since this is the case, it's used to monitor system log files, operating system audit trails, stored configuration files, and identify any activity aimed at breaching system security, such as attempted log in attempts modification of system files, creation of new processes, and so on. Local events can be identified as well as unidentified intrusions using a host-based intrusion detection system. One of the characteristics of HIDS is that they are designed to run on one host and hence need more administrative work to configure and install in numerous systems. As a result, direct attacks and Denial of Service (DoS) attacks are more prevalent for HIDS, leading to increased vulnerability. An improved form of HIDS known as Application-based IDS (AIDS) looks for programme intrusion by evaluating the application-generated files, including the execution of the free file, using anti-forensic techniques such outside the user's authorization, etc. Therefore, in order to notify end users about the encrypted network packets, it is essential to place an AIDS warning on the interface between the programme and the user.

2.4.2 Network-based IDS

Network-based IDS is an inactive tool that lies within an organization's system or network system and monitors network traffic in and out to show intrusiveness[10]. NIDS detects threats by inbound and outbound network traffic capturing and analysing. If NIDS identifies any invasive attempt, it instantly raises the alarm and notifies system administrators of such malicious efforts to take adequate measures. A NIDS can be placed at the router border to watch how traffic goes into and out of the network system. Thus, the smallest amount of monitoring units for a large network can be deployed without affecting any of the regular operations of the network system. The intrusion detection system for the network is also not likely to try direct infiltration. But network traffic, which can detect encrypted packets and fail to discriminate between distinct attack operations, can overwhelm it.

2.5 Detection Approaches

Intrusion detection systems may be generally grouped into three types according to the method of detection.

2.5.1 Anomaly-based IDS

Anomaly-based detection develops a typical network traffic statistical model that specifies the usual baseline profile model and identifies any behaviour that significantly differs. The anomaly detection tackles the problem by searching for deviations from the standard baseline model in the data under study, which enable anomaly to detect new forms of assault, can result in a significant number of false alarms since normal behaviour varies greatly, and it is sometimes difficult to describe the typical conduct in full. The anomalous approach tried to separate aberrant activity from user behaviour; an alarm was issued to the system administrator if the behaviour observed differed from the baseline profile. However, these detection approaches still have significant defects. A poor detection rate for known attacks and a high false positiveness rate, for example, misclassifies regular Network Traffic as an abnormal activity and provides an annoying alert to the manager.

2.5.2 Signature-based IDS

Based on signatures, IDS is based on pattern-based algorithms to match known attack signatures with those of the examined data using a database of available attack signatures. Thus, IDS is also called Misuse-based detection. In the misuse approach, observed actions were matched to a predefined attack signature, and if a match was discovered, an alarm was triggered. While abuse detection is highly effective in detecting known attacks, it is rendered ineffective when confronted with an unexpected or novel type of attack until the signature for that attack is revealed. As a result of the outdated signature or the absence of an attack signature, such attack actions will go unnoticed and classified as a false negative. In addition, any errors in signature definition will raise the false alarm rate, which will reduce the detection technique's effectiveness. Signature Based, which aim to find patterns indicative of previously known attacks. The advantage of such a method is to create signatures that are faster than anomaly detection for known threats. However, due to its limitations in terms of network packet congestion, costly processing resources for signature matching, and a high false-negative rate, research into anomaly detection techniques has been conducted.

2.6 Techniques

Different techniques exist to perform intrusion detection. Some of them are the following.

2.6.1 Machine Learning Technique

Machine Learning techniques create a mathematical model of sample data known as the 'training data' to forecast and categorise intrusion[3]. Machine learning techniques are utilised in many applications such as network intrusion detection, email filtering, image processing, and computer vision. Artificial neural networks (ANNs), based on biological, animal brain-based neural networks. artificial neural networks (ANNs) The neural network provides a framework for the operation of several distinct machine learning algorithms to analyse complicated data inputs. Through example consideration, such systems "learn" to do tasks usually without being designed with task-specific rules[7]. Support Vector Machines (SVM) are the related supervised learning approaches that are utilised for classification and prediction[36] and support Vector

Machines (SVM), which are also known as vector networks support networks. Machine learning methos are supervised, including a number of training samples, each labelled as one of two categories. An SVM training algorithm develops a model that shows if an incursion is inside one or the other group. A Bayesian network, which is also known to be a faith network, is a graphical probabilistic model representing a random variability set using a directed acyclic graph (DAG)[36] and is conditionally dependent on its autonoms. Genetic algorithm (GA) is a search and heuristic approach that emulates the natural selection process, utilising methods like mutation, crossover and genetic algorithms to produce the genotypes in order to get a solution to a given problem[36]. The algorithm is genetic.

2.6.2 Deep Learning Technique

Deep learning is an integral element of machine learning. The training approach can be observed, partially monitored or unattended[9]. Deep-learning architectures, including deep neural networks, deep belief, and recurrent neural networks were used for intrusion, with results comparable and often superior to those of human professionals. Deep learning techniques are used in computer vision, speech recognition, natural language processing, sound recognition, social network filtering, machine translation, bioinformatics, medical image analysis, materials inspection, and board game programs[2].

The deep neural networks is a multi-layered artificial neural neural network(ANN) compared to the rest of neural networks. First, to transform the input into the output, either linear or non-linear, the DNN discovers the right mathematical combinations. Then, by calculating probability movements across the layers the network models discover acceptable output. CNN or ConvNet are also known to be convolutional neural networks. It is a sort of deep neural network . A CNN is formed by features using 2D convolution layers, making it easy for 2D data to be processed, such as assaults. Another benefit of the CNN is that the manual extraction procedure is removed, so characteristics needed to categorise the assaults do not have to be manually identified. CNN is utilised straight from the data source to extract features. The required functionality is not pretrained; it is learnt when an image collection is shown in the network. This automatic function extraction makes deep learning models extremely precise for computer vision applications such as categorising objects. In Boltzmann Restricted Machines, each node is linked to each other node on the Boltzmann machine. There is an undirected connection between all nodes. For actual machine learning problems[10], the Boltzmann machine has not been proved helpful. By imposing specific limitations, the Boltzmann machine may be made efficient. Both visible layer and hidden layer are limited like no intralayer connectivity. All visible nodes are linked to all nodes. This is also an asymmetrical, bi-part graph with RBM two layers: visible layer and a concealed layer.

2.7 Related Works

Many experiments have been carried out to protect information systems from unwanted intrusion. Despite this, more study is required to ensure the long-term viability of network-based information systems (both wired and wireless). Advances in network communication technologies are linked to increased network activity and the growth of network assaults such as Denial of Service (DoS) attacks, worms, virus exploits, and other types of attacks. For this reason, network operators and managers must shoulder challenging responsibilities to keep the Internet accessible. In today's computing world, implementing adequate security measures to guard against computer and network breaches has become a vital concern. Furthermore, the number of network-based computer services has risen substantially, as has the number of programmes operating on networked computers. Network-based intrusion detection uses rule-based and anomaly-based methods. The goal of efficient (based) detection is to accurately identify previously identified incursions based on patterns found in data. While the rule-based method is based on rules that recognize current invaders, it does not create many false alarms due to the rules not knowing new intruders. Analyzing and reporting abnormal computational behavioural patterns is part of anomaly detection. Concerning anomaly-based detection, models of expected system behaviour can be constructed from the observed data and differentiate between significant deviations and exceptions. To detect anomalies, one must look for atypical behaviour that does not fit the norm. the anomaly detection technique can assess new or undetected intrusions Organisations are increasingly seeking solutions to these problems to protect their brand. Installing an intrusion detection system is a more secure option (IDS). Because these systems now rely on signatures of the assault used to identify an intruder or changes in the System's behavioural patterns, they now rely on the intruder's attack to function. The attackers are prepared to grasp these systems, which are either signature-based or anomaly-based. When the existing IDS cannot recognise an attack because it does not match the attack signatures currently defined, this scenario arises. Table 2.1 represents no. of papers categorise as per detection technique like Machine learning, Deep learning and combined techniques. Table 2.2 gives no. of papers considered for review year wise. Table 2.3 gives details of papers categorize as per Classification techniques like Neural Network, CNN, DNN etc. Figure 2.3 depicts no. of papers per algorithm studied for survey, this pie chart indicates mostly researchers tries to used CNN.

Table 2.1: Papers categorise as per detection technique

Algorithms		Papers	Paper Nos.
Machine Learning		24	[1 – 9] [22] [14 – 38] [40] [41] [45] [46] [49] [53 – 61] [63 – 69] [71 – 73]
Deep Learning		48	[18] [19] [23] [38] [42–44] [52] [62] [74 – 84]
Machine Learning	+	4	[47] [48] [50] [51] [70]
Deep Learning			

Table 2.2: Papers categorise as per year wise

Year	AIDS	SIDS	Combined	Total papers
2018-2022	57	4	2	63
2013-2017	11	5	2	18
1993-2012	8	20	3	31

Table 2.3: Papers categorize as per Classification techniques

Sr. No.	Algorithm	No. of Papers	Reference papers
1	Neural Network	9	[16] [48] [53] [57] [58 [84 [106] [127] [128]
2	Convolution Neural Network	17	[14] [18] [19] [20] [21] [28] [29] [31] [32] [33] [35] [41] [56] [61] [64]
3	Deep Neural Network	14	[13] [27] [28] [30] [34] [40] [49] [50] [57] [59] [64] [65] [73] [77]
4	Auto Encoder	13	[26] [28] [33] [37] [38] [42] [44] [51] [54] [62] [64] [67] [68]
5	Deep Belief Network	3	[41] [55] [75]
6	Long Short term memory	3	[32] [61] [65]
7	Self-taught learning	2	[54] [77]
8	Self organizing Maps	2	[81] [85]
9	Support Vector Machine	7	[18] [51] [54] [55] [70] [74] [79]
10	Genetic Algorithm	9	[52] [48] [70] [79] [89] [90] [94] [95] [125]
11	Logistic Regression	2	[22] [84]
12	Decision Tree	12	[15] [56] [70] [74] [78] [80] [101] [105] [113] [122] [123] [124]
13	Naive Bayes	7	[43] [52] [54] [74] [82] [99] [110]
14	Random Forest	4	[42] [48] [52] [95]
15	K Mean clustering	1	[42]
16	Recurrent Neural Network	3	[57] [67] [68]
17	Data mining	4	[99] [101] [108] [116]
18	Others	20	[5] [19] [10] [21] [23] [43] [49] [52] [59] [62] [80]
			[84] [92] [93] [100] [104] [105] [106] [107] [108]

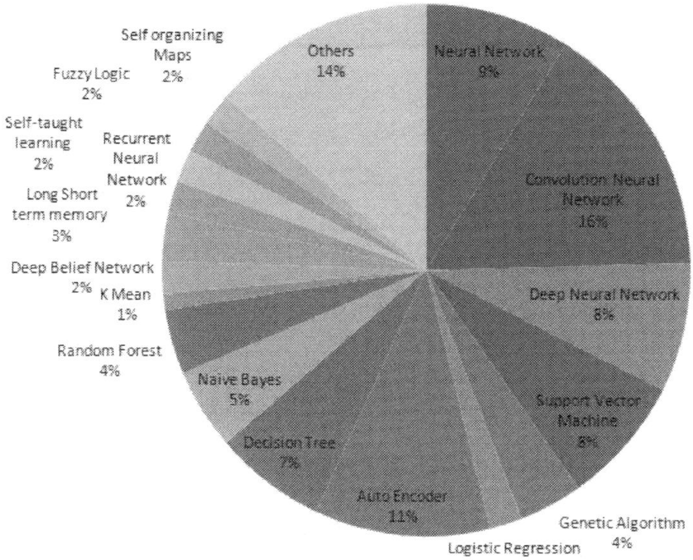

Figure 2.3: Algorithm based papers: Survey

2.8 Background of IDS

2.8.1 Anomaly Based IDS

Anomaly-based IDS detected new kind of attacks. The aberrant behaviour has been detected. The detection of anomalies defines the network performance that should be anticipated. Any major changes in these outlines' performance are flagged as potential attacks[7]. It aims to detect malicious traffic by looking for deviations from trusted typical traffic patterns [8]. Detailed survey of AIDS is given in Table2.4 where it includes author name, year of publication, technique used for building IDS, learning technique used, dataset used and attacks covered.

Advantages:

1. Anomaly-based IDS are able to detect new attacks .
2. IDS identify attacks when entire attack information is not available.
3. There have to be no restrictions to write [16].

Disadvantages:

1. It produce a high rate of false alarms.
2. It's hard to define a rule set from AIDS.
3. The nature of the attack is not defined[16].

This section reviews the literature for network intrusion detection systems based on anomaly based IDS which uses machine learning and deep learning methodologies.

Two-level classification by W. Seo et.al.[17] simultaneously yielded excellent results and real-time detection. Classifiers at levels one and two were in use on the corporate level. Incoming data traffic was detected with middling accuracy using a first-level classifier. After that, the classifier at level two used traffic flow statistics to make an accurate classification. Machine-based anomaly models, such as the support machine model developed by Duo et. al. [18], have been developed (SVM). SVM kernel parameters are optimised via vector optimisation (PSO-SVM) and genetic algorithm assistance (GA-SVM). The second aspect to note is that random forests were used to generate two separate models for various assault types in this essay. The three ID3 dichotomies are all iterative (CART). The next stage is to examine the construction of the intrusion detection and attack classification model using the public data set KDD-99 and the real-time Ethernet simulation train data set. S. Ho et al. [19] present a Convolutional Neural Network (CNN) approach for developing an IDS system. In order to detect network intruders, the proposed IDS paradigm classifies all network packets into benign or malicious categories. Using data from CICIDS2017, the model was tested and improved upon.

Jiarui Man et al.[20] describe a residual learning-based NIDS model. Deeper Convolutional neural networks(CNN) with residual blocks are constructed after the UNSW-NB15 data set is converted into visuals to learn more critical attributes. To address the class imbalance issue in the training set and detect modest attacks in the testing set, the modified focal loss is used in place of the cross-entropy loss function.

The XGBoost-DNN model was developed by Devan P. Khare et al.[21] utilising the NSL-KDD Dataset and the XGBoost feature extraction method to detect network interference. Later, a deep neural network (DNN) was employed for feature selection, normalisation, and classification. Binary was the only format that worked.

Long-term ensemble learning was proposed by X. Li et al[22]. They developed multi-class regression models based on probability performance and classified training data by attack type using ensemble-based learning.

M. H. Haghighat et al. [23] recently published a novel neural network-based deep learning system based on voting. Deep learning frameworks may be used to a wide range of problems.

To improve the reliability and robustness of the findings, you may use a voting-based Neural Network to combine the best models developed by numerous data features and several deep learning architectures. As a consequence, VNN is an important tool for security experts who may use it to spot increasingly complex attacks. On two well-known and extensively used datasets, the voting method was shown to be effective in improving machine efficiency, with false alarms decreased by up to 75%.

In their study, F. Z. Belgrana et al. [24] using the Condensed Nearest Neighbors (CoNN) method. It was a great tool for classification and regression because it considered sample dispersion. Condensed Nearest Neighbors reduces the size of the data vector while maintaining good attack detection performance, which leads to more efficient device resource usage and quicker processing. They also trained their learning data set using a neural network (NN). To highlight the effectiveness of their methods, they compared them to K Nearest Neighbors (KNN) approaches.

X. Zhang et al. [25] explained a Convolution Neural Network based intrusion detection system. Prior to training, SMOTE and Edited Nearest were employed to balance network traffic. The system was evaluated using the NSL-KDD Dataset. The accuracy of this IDS model is 83.31 percent. S. Park et al. [26] developed a character-level binary image manipulation anomaly-based approach and convolutional autoencoder (CAE) for Hyper Text Transfer Protocol communications. Asymmetric CNN make comprise the CAE's encoding and decoding sides,

respectively[28]. Additionally, the CAE tries to create a related image when a message-transformed image is supplied to it. For everyday communications, the CAE was trained to decrease the binary cross-entropy (BCE) in the input and output pictures. The suggested method recognises an aberrant message when, after sufficient training, the BCE of a message is more than a certain threshold value.

H. Zhou et al. [28] propose a deep learning-based technique for Intrusion identification. Both a worm identification system based on convolutional neural networks and a worm signature generation system based on deep neural networks are required (DNN). Using CNN to train the worm detection model is an excellent strategy. Before producing the signature of a DNN-based worm, the model is trained on how to extract and identify payloads and signatures in a worm payload using a DNN training module[29]. This approach is then used to produce the

DNN-based signature. The worm payload and signatures acquired from it are used as the training input by DNN. The worm signature is formed when the worms are injected in a test word into the qualified DNN model, according to the selected search strategy for Signature. A hybrid and deep hierarchical intrusion detection network technique was presented by Jiang et al. [30]. It use one-sided selection (OSS) to delete the bulk of the noise sample, then Synthetic Minority sampling to get the greatest number of minority samples (SMOTE). The model may get a better grasp of the features of minority samples while lowering the amount of time it takes to exercise by using this method. It initially collects geographical information using CNN (neural networks) and a Bi-directional Long-Term Memory to produce a hierarchical network model (Bi-LTM).

A deep learning strategy was created by M. Azizjon et al. [32] for creating scalable and efficient IDS (1D-CNN). In the realm of computer vision, two-dimensional CNN algorithms have demonstrated great performance in object recognition in images. The Softmax classification was used to classify network intrusions while the Adam optimiser maximises learning rate during DNN training. In a distributed environment with cooperative intelligent agents scattered throughout the Internet, DIDS [33] was developed (s). In this study, three various fuzzy rule-based classifiers for detecting network intrusions are examined. The outcomes of support vector machines, decision trees, and linear genetic programming have been compared to those of other machine learning techniques. In order to replicate IDS, they also simulated Distributed Soft Computing-based IDS (D-SCIDS), which is a group of classifiers.

Xiao et al.[34] proposed CNN–IDS, which uses Lenet-5's conventional CNN model to identify intrusions. For optimization, LeNet was utilised to enhance network format and batch normalisation was performed (BN).

Recurrent neural networks (RNN) and convolutional neural networks (CNN) in LuNet efficiently extract temporal and spatial information by training incoming traffic packet data in real-time as granularity increases. P. Wu et al.[35] developed LuNet, a hierarchical neural network that integrates CNN and RNN. They found that LuNet maintains a high degree of detection capabilities and has a low percentage of false-positive alarms using their results from two network traffic datasets[36].

A unique neural network intrusion detection system (IDS) is proposed by Y. Xiao et al. [39].

(CNN-IDS). Dimensionality reduction techniques are used early in the data processing pipeline to remove redundant and redundant network traffic characteristics. The CNN automatically pulls features from low-dimensional data, and supervised learning retrieves more trustworthy intrusion detection data. Before testing the recommended CNN model on the KDD-CUP99 test data set, the researcher converts the original traffic vector data to an image format to save time and money on computation.

The Kyoto, WSN-DS, NSL-KDD, UNSW-NB15, and CICIDS 2017 datasets are used by Vinayakumar et al. [40] to construct a scalable and effective IDS that employs a deep neural network (DNN) to recognise unknown and unidentified intrusions.

In the framework of NSL-KDD, Quamar Niyaz et al. [45] developed the Self-taught Learning (STL) based deep learning technique.

A practical detection approach for DDOS and DOS attacks was created by Benamar Bouyeddou et al. [65] using statistical and exponential smoothing (ES) measurements from Continuous Graded Probability Score (CRPS). The distinction between a traffic finding and a typical transmission is determined by the CRPS. The CRPS Exponentially Smoothing Scheme was used to detect deviations since it was sensitive to tiny alterations. The non-symmetric deep auto-encoder, a deep learning-based technique for extracting unsupervised characteristics for intrusion detection, was reported by Nathan Shone et al.[67] (NDAE). The NDAE looked at the current methodologies' feasibility and long-term viability. They also demonstrated NDAEs placed on top of one another. The NSL-KDD and KDD Cup '99 datasets, which were developed in GPU-enabled TensorFlow, were utilised for classifier validation. Anomalies were discovered using the CRPS-ES approach using a non-parameterized decision threshold created via kernel density estimation. To identify anomalies in HTTP connections, S. Park et al. [68] presented a CAE-level binary image transformation as part of a Convolutionary-autonomous (CAE) binary image-level transformation character. CAE employs the CNN symmetrical encoder and decoder, as well as the CNN symmetrical structural encoder and decoder. When converting a photo to a message, CAE expects the same result. Binary cross-entropy (BCE), which can occur between input and output images, is prevented using CAE.J. Jabez et al.[76] provided an outlier detection approach that evaluated the anomaly dataset using the Neighborhood Outlier Factor (NOF). To increase the performance of the Intrusion Detection System, the trained model makes advantage of massive datasets and a distributed storage architecture.

K. Hwang et al. [83] suggested merging the ADS and SNORT approaches for a weighted signature creation strategy by extracting signatures from irregularities found. HIDS collected signatures from ADS output and added them to the SNORT signature database for speedy and precise intrusion detection. A method was developed by F. Hussain and associates [123] for transforming network traffic data into picture formats. The widely used CNN model ResNet was then trained using the modified data. A full review of the literature on anomaly-based IDS provided in Table 2.4.

Table 2.4: Literature review of Anomaly based IDS

Sr. No.	Author Name	Year	Technique	Learning Techniques	Dataset	Attacks Covered
1	Rani M. et. al. [5]	2022	Deep learning	deep neural network	NSL KDD UNSW15	Probing, DoS, R2L, U2R, Fuzzers, Analysis, Backdoors, DoS, Exploits, Generic, Reconnaissance, Shellcode and Worms
2	Jian Yu et. al.[6]	2022	Deep learning	multi-scale convolutional neural network	NSL KDD	Probing, DoS, R2L, U2R
3	Wei Wang[7]	2022	Deep Learning	Neural Network for object Representation Learning	NSL-KDD and AWIDS	Probing, DoS, R2L, U2R, Deauth, Disas, Krack, Kr001,SSH, Botnet, Malware, SQL Injection, SSDP, Website sppofing
4	R. V. Mendonca et al [8]	2021	Deep learning	Hierarchical Tree-CNN algorithm activated by Soft-Root-Sign	NSL KDD	Probing, DoS, R2L, U2R

Sr. No.	Author Name	Year	Technique	Learning Techniques	Dataset	Attacks Covered
5	W. Seo et al. [17]	2021	Deep learning	Two-level classifier	UNSW- NB15 CICIDS2017	Fuzzers, Analysis, Backdoors, DoS, Exploits, Generic, Reconnaissance, Shellcode , Worms and DDOS, PortScan, Bot, Infiltration, Brute Force, SQL Injection, Cross site Scripting, Transfer protocol Patator, Secure Shell Patator, DoS Golden Eye , DoS Hulk
6	Duo et al. [18]	2021	Deep learning	Particle Swarm Optimisation(PSO),Genetic algorithm support vector machines (GA-SVM)	KDD 99	Probing, DoS, R2L, U2R
7	S. Ho et al. [19]	2021	Deep learning	Convolutional Neural Network	CICIDS 2017	DDOS, PortScan, Bot, Infiltration, Brute Force, SQL Injection, Cross site Scripting, Transfer protocol Patator, Secure Shell Patator, DoS Golden Eye , DoS Hulk

Sr. No.	Author Name	Year	Technique	Learning Techniques	Dataset	Attacks Covered
8	Jiarui Man,[20]	2021	Deep Learning	ResNet CNN	UNSW	Fuzzers, Analysis, Backdoors, DoS, Exploits, Generic, Reconnaissance, Shellcode and Worms
9	Devan, P., Khare, [21]	2021	Deep Learning	CNN	CICIDS2017	DDOS, PortScan, Bot, Infiltration, Brute Force, SQL Injection, Cross site Scripting, Transfer protocol Patator, Secure Shell Patator, DoS Golden Eye , DoS Hulk
10	X. Li et al.,[22]	2021	Machine Learning	Multi-class regression models, long-term ensemble learning	NSL KDD	Probing, DoS, R2L, U2R
11	M. H. Haghighat [23]	2021	Machine Learning	Condensed Nearest Neighbors (CoNN) algorithm	NSL-KDD	Probing, DoS, R2L, U2R

Sr. No.	Author Name	Year	Technique	Learning Techniques	Dataset	Attacks Covered
12	F. Z. Belgrana, [24]	2020	Machine Learning	Continuous Graded Probability Score (CRPS)	DARPA99, MAWI and ICMPv6	DDOS, PortScan, Bot, Infiltration, Brute Force, SQL Injection, Cross site Scripting, Transfer protocol Patator, Secure Shell Patator, DoS Golden Eye , DoS Hulk, smurf, nmap, ipsweep, nmap
13	Karatas et al[25]	2020	Machine Learning	Synthetic Minority Over Sampling	CSECIC-IDS2018	DDOS, PortScan, Bot, Infiltration, Brute Force, SQL Injection, Cross site Scripting, Transfer protocol Patator, Secure Shell Patator, DoS Golden Eye , DoS Hulk
14	Yang et al[26]	2020	Deep Learning	Adversarial Supervised Variational Auto Encoder with Deep Neural Network	NSL-KDD	Probing, DoS, R2L, U2R
15	Sangkatsanee et al.[27]	2020	Machine Learning	Apache Spark Big Data Classifier	KDD99	Probing, DoS, R2L, U2R
16	Yu et al [28]	2020	Deep Learning	Deep neural Network and CNN	NSL-KDD	Probing, DoS, R2L, U2R

Sr. No.	Author Name	Year	Technique	Learning Techniques	Dataset	Attacks Covered
17	Andresini et al [29]	2020	Deep Learning	Multistage Auto Encoder and CNN	NSL-KDD	Probing, DoS, R2L, U2R
18	H. Zhou [30]	2020	Deep Learning	XGBoost–DNN model	NSL-KDD	Probing, DoS, R2L, U2R
19	K. Jiang, [31]	2020	Deep Learning	Convolutional neural network (CNN) with automated Signature generation	NSL KDD	Probing, DoS, R2L, U2R
20	M. Azizjon, [32]	2020	Deep Learning	CNN to pull out characteristics and a BiLSTM	NSL-KDD and UNSW-NB15	Probing, DoS, R2L, U2R , Fuzzers, Analysis, Backdoors, DoS, Exploits, Generic, Reconnaissance, Shellcode and Worms
21	R. Vinayakumar, [33]	2020	Deep Learning	Two-dimensional CNN	UNSW NB15	Fuzzers, Analysis, Backdoors, DoS, Exploits, Generic, Reconnaissance, Shellcode and Worms

Sr. No.	Author Name	Year	Technique	Learning Techniques	Dataset	Attacks Covered
22	Y. Xiao, [34]	2019	Deep Learning	deep neural network (DNN)	UNSW-NB15, NSL-KDD, WSN-DS, Kyoto, and CICIDS 2017	Fuzzers, Analysis, Backdoors, DoS, Exploits, Generic, Reconnaissance, Shellcode and Worms DDOS, PortScan, Bot, Infiltration, Brute Force, SQL Injection, Cross site Scripting, Transfer protocol Patator, Secure Shell Patator, DoS Golden Eye , DoS Hulk
23	P. Wu and H. Guo [35]	2019	Deep Learning	CNN model of Lenet-5	KDDcup99	Probing, DoS, R2L, U2R
24	X. Zhang, [36]	2019	Deep Learning	CNN with SMOTE coupled with Edited Neares	NSL KDD	Probing, DoS, R2L, U2R
25	Papamartizivanous et al[37]	2019	Deep learning	Sparse Auto Encoder-Based Self-Learning	NSLKDD, KDD Cup'99	Probing, DoS, R2L, U2R

Sr. No.	Author Name	Year	Technique	Learning Techniques	Dataset	Attacks Covered
26	Khan et al [38]	2019	Deep Learning	A Stacked Auto Encoder model with two stages.	KDD Cup'99 UNSW-NB15	Probing, DoS, R2L, U2R , Fuzzers, Analysis, Backdoors, DoS, Exploits, Generic, Reconnaissance, Shellcode and Worms
27	Xiao et al[39]	2019	Deep Learning	Convolutional Neural Network	KDD Cup'99	Probing, DoS, R2L, U2R
28	Vinayakumar et al[40]	2019	Deep Learning	Deep Neural Network	NSL-KDD	Probing, DoS, R2L, U2R
29	Wei et al [41]	2019	Deep Learning	Deep Belief Network	NSL-KDD	Probing, DoS, R2L, U2R
30	Zhang et al [42]	2019	Deep Learning	Variational AutoEncoder (VAE)	UNSW-NB15 CICIDS2017	DDOS, PortScan, Bot, Infiltration, Brute Force, SQL Injection, Cross site Scripting, Transfer protocol Patator, Secure Shell Patator, DoS Golden Eye , DoS Hulk, Fuzzers, Analysis, Backdoors, DoS, Exploits, Generic, Reconnaissance, Shellcode and Worms

Sr. No.	Author Name	Year	Technique	Learning Techniques	Dataset	Attacks Covered
31	Quamar Niyaz [45],	2019	Deep Learning	CNN model of Lenet-5	KDD-CUP99	Probing, DoS, R2L, U2R
32	A. Dawoud [63]	2018	Deep learning	Restricted Boltzmann machine with Software Defined Networking	KDDCUP 99	Probing, DoS, R2L, U2R
33	Yao et.al. [46]	2018	Machine Learning	Random Forest ,K-Means Clustering	KDD Cup'99	Probing, DoS, R2L, U2R
34	Shen et al[47]	2018	Machine learning	Ensemble Method with Optimization	NSL-KDD, KDD Cup'99, Kyoto,	Probing, DoS, R2L, U2R
35	Kunal e.al. [43]	2019	Machine Learning	C 4.5 Decision Tree and Naive Bayes Classifier	KDD Cup 99	Probing, DoS, R2L, U2R
36	Malaiya et al [44]	2019	Deep Learning	Variational AutoEncoder (VAE)	NSL-KDD	Probing, DoS, R2L, U2R
37	Ali et. al[48]	2018	Machine learning	An algorithm based on particle swarms and a neural network	KDD Cup'99	Probing, DoS, R2L, U2R

Sr. No.	Author Name	Year	Technique	Learning Techniques	Dataset	Attacks Covered
38	Jia et. al0[49]	2018	Deep Learning	Deep Neural Network	KDD cup'99 and NSLKDD	Probing, DoS, R2L, U2R
39	Wang et. al[50]	2018	Deep Learning	Deep Neural Network	NSLKDD	Probing, DoS, R2L, U2R
40	Yan et. al[51]	2018	Machine Learning and Deep learning	Using SVM with Sparse Auto Encoding	NSL-KDD	Probing, DoS, R2L, U2R
41	Naseer et. al[52]	2018	Deep learning and Machine Learning	Naive bays, decision trees, random forests, quadratic discriminant analysis	NSL-KDD	Probing, DoS, R2L, U2R
42	A. Shenfield [58]	2018	Deep learning	Artificial neural network	Snort and Sguil alert data	others

Sr. No.	Author Name	Year	Technique	Learning Techniques	Dataset	Attacks Covered
43	Xu et. al[53]	2018	Deep learning	Gated Recurrent Units are used as memory in a neural network with multiple perception layers..	KDD Cup'99 and NSL-KDD	Probing, DoS, R2L, U2R
44	Al-Qatf et. al[54]	2018	Deep learning and Machine Learning	Sparse Auto Encoder and SVM-based Self-Taught Learning Model	NSL-KDD	Probing, DoS, R2L, U2R
45	T. Tang [76]	2016	Deep learning	Deep Neural Network	NSL-KDD.	Probing, DoS, R2L, U2R
46	Marir et. al[55]	2018	Deep learning and Machine Learning	Networks such as SVM and DBN	NSL-KDD	Probing, DoS, R2L, U2R

Sr. No.	Author Name	Year	Technique	Learning Techniques	Dataset	Attacks Covered
47	Algatani et al.[56]	2018	Machine Learning	Bayasian Network, Naive Bayes classifier, Decision Tree, Random Forest,Artificial Neural Network	CICIDS17 NSL KDD	Probing, DoS, R2L, U2R, DDOS, PortScan, Bot, Infiltration, Brute Force, SQL Injection, Cross site Scripting, Transfer protocol Patator, Secure Shell Patator, DoS Golden Eye , DoS Hulk
48	H. A. Najada [57]	2018	Deep learning	Deep Neural Network	UNB ISCX IDS 2012	DDOS, PortScan, Bot, Infiltration, Brute Force, SQL Injection, Cross site Scripting, Transfer protocol Patator, Secure Shell Patator, DoS Golden Eye , DoS Hulk
49	D. Aksu [59]	2018	Deep learning	Deep Neural Network	CIC IDS 2017	DDOS, PortScan, Bot, Infiltration, Brute Force, SQL Injection, Cross site Scripting, Transfer protocol Patator, Secure Shell Patator, DoS Golden Eye , DoS Hulk

Sr. No.	Author Name	Year	Technique	Learning Techniques	Dataset	Attacks Covered
50	H. Liu [60]	2018	Deep learning	Convolutional neural network	CNTC-2017 WebShell, Darpa 1998, KDD99, CSIC 2000 http header	DDOS, PortScan, Bot, Infiltration, Brute Force, SQL Injection, Cross site Scripting, Transfer protocol Patator, Secure Shell Patator, DoS Golden Eye , DoS Hulk, smurf, nmap, ipsweep, nmap
51	B. Roy [61]	2018	Deep learning	Recurrent Neural Network , Long short term Memory for IoT	UNSW-NB15	Fuzzers, Analysis, Backdoors, DoS, Exploits, Generic, Reconnaissance, Shellcode and Worms
52	J. Yan [62]	2018	Deep learning	Multilayer perceptron, Sparse Autoencoder Support Vector Machine	NSL-KDD, UNSW- NB15	Probing, DoS, R2L, U2R ,Fuzzers, Analysis, Backdoors, DoS, Exploits, Generic, Reconnaissance, Shellcode and Worms
53	M. Al-Hawawreh [64]	2018	Deep learning	Deep auto-encoder and Deep Neural Network for IoT	NSL-KDD, UNSW- NB15	Probing, DoS, R2L, U2R , Fuzzers, Analysis, Backdoors, DoS, Exploits, Generic, Reconnaissance, Shellcode and Worms

Sr. No.	Author Name	Year	Technique	Learning Techniques	Dataset	Attacks Covered
54	F. Feng [65]	2018	Deep learning	Deep Neural Network , CNN , Long short term Memory , for ad-hoc networks	KDD CUP 99 Dos attack, Waf logs for XSS and SQL attack	Probing, DoS, R2L, U2R
55	Benamar[66]	2018	Machine Learning	Neighborhood Outlier Factor (NOF)	KDD 99	Probing, DoS, R2L, U2R
56	Shone, N [67]	2018	Deep Learning	Non-symmetric deep auto-encoder (NDAE)	NSL-KDD and KDD Cup '99	Probing, DoS, R2L, U2R
57	W. Lin, et.al [68]	2018	Deep Learning	CNN	NSL-KDD, UNSW	Probing, DoS, R2L, U2R, Fuzzers, Analysis, Backdoors, DoS, Exploits, Generic, Reconnaissance, Shellcode and Worms
58	S. Park [69]	2018	Deep Learning	convolutional autoencoder (CAE)	MNIST dataset	Fuzzers, Analysis, Backdoors, DoS, Exploits, Generic, Reconnaissance, Shellcode and Worms

Sr. No.	Author Name	Year	Technique	Learning Techniques	Dataset	Attacks Covered
59	Ajith Abraham [70]	2017	Machine Learning	Linear genetic programming , Decision trees and support vector machines	NSL KDD	Probing, DoS, R2L, U2R
60	C. Yin [71]	2017	Deep learning	Recurrent Neural Network	NSL-KDD,	Probing, DoS, R2L, U2R
61	Yin et. al[72]	2017	Deep learning	Recurrent Neural Network	NSL-KDD	Probing, DoS, R2L, U2R
62	A Diro [73]	2017	Deep learning	Deep Neural Network for IOT	NSL-KDD,	Probing, DoS, R2L, U2R
63	Tahir et.al. [74]	2016	Machine learning	Naive Baayes ,Support vector machine, Decision table Decision tree,	NSL- KDD	Probing, DoS, R2L, U2R
64	Y. Liu [75]	2016	Deep learning	Deep belief network+Restricted Boltzmann machine	NSL-KDD,	Probing, DoS, R2L, U2R

Sr. No.	Author Name	Year	Technique	Learning Techniques	Dataset	Attacks Covered
65	J. Jabez [76]	2015	Deep Learning	Self-taught Learning (STL)	NSL KDD	Probing, DoS, R2L, U2R
66	Adel Sabry et.al. [77]	2014	Machine Learning	decision tree (DT) classifier	KDD Cup 99 dataset	Probing, DoS, R2L, U2R
67	A.M.Chan dras hekhar et.al. [78]	2013	Machine learning	Fuzzy C means clustering, Support vector machine	KDD cup 1999	Probing, DoS, R2L, U2R
68	Gisung Kim et.al. [79]	2013	Machine learning	C4.5 decision tree , Support vector machine	NSL-KDD data set	Probing, DoS, R2L, U2R
69	Bose et.al. [80]	2012	Machine Learning	Self Organizing Map algorithms	KDD-cup 1999	Probing, DoS, R2L, U2R
72	Levent Koc. et.al. [81]	2012	Machine Learning	Hidden Naïve Bayes (HNB) model	KDD-cup 1999	Probing, DoS, R2L, U2R

Sr. No.	Author Name	Year	Technique	Learning Techniques	Dataset	Attacks Covered
70	Muna et.al [82]	2010	Machine Learning	Hybrid fuzzy logic and neural network	DARPA	smurf, nmap, ipsweep, nmap , smurf, nmap, ipsweep, nmap
71	Min Seok et.al. [83]	2010	Machine Learning	logistic regression mode	KDD-cup 1999	Probing, DoS, R2L, U2R
72	Gao et. al[84]	2009	Machine Learning	Algorithms that combine machine learning with voting	NSL-KDD	Probing, DoS, R2L, U2R
73	M. Bahrololum et.al. [85]	20009	Machine learning	NN based on Self Organizing Map (SOM)	KDD-cup 1999	Probing, DoS, R2L, U2R
74	K. Ilgun[87]	1993	Machine Learning	State transition analysis	Audit trails	other

2.8.2 Signature based IDS

Signature based IDS is also known as misuse or rule-based IDS. Misuse-based IDS is a kind of intrusion detection system that detects known assaults. The database contains the signatures of each known attack, and the incoming data is compared against the signatures of the attacks[5]. Detailed survey of SIDS is given in table2.5 where it includes author name, year of publication, technique used for building IDS, dataset used and attacks covered.

An IDS based on signature services is employed when someone sends data over the network. As packets enter the IDS, it gathers information while searching the Ruleset for a certain pattern. [5].

Advantages:

1. Whenever the signatures match, an alert is triggered off.
2. Network behaviour and specified rules are used to build signatures.
3. Low formation of false positive alarms.

Disadvantages

1. The database can only identify attacks that have previously been saved.
2. Human attacks that are made in real time cannot be identified.

Intrusion Detection Systems (IDSs) frequently use websites that feed them new threat signatures or administrators manually updating databases. According to Mutep Y Al et al. [91], automating attack lists may be accomplished by using a filtering system that also functions as a secondary IDS engine. Similarities are used to create new attack signatures, and an IDS blacklist of IP factors automates the update of the IDS database without the need for human input. By comparing fewer signatures, H. Almutairi and N. T. Abdelmajeed [92] found that the time required to validate signatures was reduced. Instead of being deleted in rare instances, the infrequent signatures are kept in a separate database. Two remote databases are used to hold both newly arriving traffic and previously scanned files, while a third database is also being updated simultaneously. If a match appears in any database, the search is stopped. In order to avoid replacing frequent signatures with uncommon or benign signatures, the signature update operation should follow the guidelines mentioned in the preceding section.

According to the Pinem et al[93]research team, companies may choose to install several S-IDS in order to protect themselves against security breaches. If all packets in a specific flow can be monitored to identify intrusion fingerprints, each of these systems can function independently.New technologies that use many channels to increase network performance, like Multi-Path TCP, will unavoidably cause issues. Malicious payloads may be dispersed across several channels in order to evade detection by signature-based network intrusion detection systems. The deployment of many monitors prevents the detection of an intrusion signature since none of them gives a complete picture of network activity. This asynchronous online precise string matching problem formalises and solves the distributed signature-based intrusion detection issue. As a group, the employees of W. Yassin [94] used a novel Signature-Based Anomaly Detection Scheme (SADS) to better examine and identify network packet headers in their investigation. Using classifier mining techniques like Naive Bayes and Random Forest to mix different types of data, including false alarm data and detection outcomes, can reduce the frequency of false alarms and create signatures based on detection findings to accelerate future prediction processing. Many studies based on DARPA data sets from 1999 to 2012 have shown that SADS is more effective and takes less time to process than previous anomaly-based detection systems. In order to better identify intrusion fingerprints, S. Mabu et.al. [98] used an entirely new technique. Two signature-based network intrusion detection systems, each running the Snort software and given rules and packets, have been shown in trials to reduce detection times of hostile traffic. Table 2.5 gives detailed literature review of Signature based IDS. The data-parallel approach proposed by Sadoddin et al.[99] will enable Snort to reduce packet processing time while increasing detection rates. In addition, our System is expandable both horizontally and vertically, allowing us to add and remove hosts as needed.

Al-Mamory et.al [100] tested 356 created Snort rules in this work, which is an in-depth investigation of severe SNIDS Snort assaults. This article investigates. Theoretically, there are 173 such attacks, of which 183 are null-day assaults. According to the study, Snort can discover zero-day vulnerabilities (a mean of 17 percent detection). When an attack is known to have occurred, the detection rate tends to be much greater (a mean of 54 percent detection). Null days may be discovered, manufactured, and evaded, according to a new research that delves into detail.

Machine learning clustering is used by Kruegel C. and Toth T. [108] to enhance matching. Due to the large number of signatures, a decision tree is developed to identify potentially risky scenarios with the fewest recurring comparisons feasible . An extensive experimental investigation revealed that the detection process has significantly improved even when the present Snort detector engine is contrasted with the most recent detector upgrade.

Kruegel et al. [113] designed a decision tree that decreases the amount of comparisons that are unnecessary. In this paper, the Kruegel approach is enhanced by modifying the decision-making tree clustering algorithm.

Table 2.5: Literature review of Signature based IDS

Sr. No	Author	Year	Detection Technique	Datasets	Attack types
1	J. Liu et.al.[87]	2020	Genetic algorithm with fuzzy	CICIDS2017 data set	DDOS, PortScan, Bot, Infiltration, Brute Force, SQL Injection, Cross site Scripting, Transfer protocol Patator, Secure Shell Patator, DoS Golden Eye , DoS Hulk
2	Almseidin et.al. [88]	2019	Fuzzy rule	open source DDOS dataset	UDP Flood, ICMP Floods, SYN floods, Ping of death , Smurf DDOS
3	Boonyopakorn et.al. [89]	2019	Fuzzy association rules	10% data sets of KDD cup 99 data sets	Probing, DoS, R2L, U2R
4	Mutep et.al. [90]	2019	Using a filtering engine, update	Attack signatures (EmergingThreats.com)	others

Sr. No	Author	Year	Detection Technique	Datasets	Attack types
5	H. Almutairi[91]	2017	Small databases containing the most common signatures and an updating agent are used in paral lel processing.	—	others
7	Pinem et.al.[92]	2015	Classification and regression tree	KDD Cup 1999 dataset	Probing, DoS, R2L, U2R
8	W. Yassin[93]	2014	Naive Bayes and Random Forest	DARPA 1999 and ISCX 2012	smurf, nmap, ipsweep, nmap , smurf, nmap, ipsweep, nmap, Brute force, SSH, Infiltrating, HttpDoS, DDOS, Brute force, SSH, Infiltrating, HttpDoS, DDOS
9	Benferhat et.al. [94]	2013	Bayesian networks model for classifying the alarms	Webtraffic dataset	web based attacks
10	Phuong Do[95]	2013	Snort Using Decision Tree	Snort Rules	attacks from Snort ruleset
11	Elshoush et.al. [96]	2012	Knowledge-based correlation	DARPA 2000 Datasets	Webtraffic dataset

Sr. No	Author	Year	Detection Technique	Datasets	Attack types
12	Mabu et.al.[97]	2011	Fuzzy class association rule mining using genetic	KDD99Cup and DARPA98	smurf, nmap, ipsweep, nmap , smurf, nmap, ipsweep, nmap, Probing, DoS, R2L, U2R
13	Sadoddin et.al.[98]	2009	a real time alarm classification scheme based on frequent structured patterns	DARPA2000 Dataset	smurf, nmap, ipsweep, nmap , smurf, nmap, ipsweep, nmap
14	Al-Mamory et.al. [99]	2009	alarm mining and various correlation algorithms	KDD CUP99 Dataset	Probing, DoS, R2L, U2R
15	Soleimani et.al. [100]	2008	Decision tree	Snort	attacks from Snort ruleset
16	Thomas et.al. [101]	2008	neural network based alarm classification technique	DARPA 99	smurf, nmap, ipsweep, nmap , smurf, nmap, ipsweep, nmap
16	Massicotte et.al. [102]	2007	signature is monitoring any attempted cases of logging in as root to a UNIX machine	Snort	Snort Ruleset
17	Maggi et.al. [103]	2007	Statistical tests for alert correlation	DARPA	smurf, nmap, ipsweep, nmap , smurf, nmap, ipsweep, nmap

Sr. No	Author	Year	Detection Technique	Datasets	Attack types
18	Brunley et.al. [104]	2006	Vulnerability signature Vulnerability signature with signature generation	–	-
19	Pietraszek et.al. [105]	2005	hybrid of two approaches – one part comprises data mining and the other part tunes the signature engine to reflect the learnt behavior.	DARPA1999	smurf, nmap, ipsweep, nmap , smurf, nmap, ipsweep, nmap
20	D. Yu et.al. [106]	2004	knowledge base of target network to correlate alarms	DARPA	smurf, nmap, ipsweep, nmap , smurf, nmap, ipsweep, nmap
21	Kruegel C et.al. [107]	2003	Decision Tree	NSL KDD DARPA 1999 and ISCX 2012	smurf, nmap, ipsweep, nmap , smurf, nmap, ipsweep, nmap, Brute force, SSH, Infiltrating, HttpDoS, DDOS,
22	Sommer et.al. [108]	2003	contextual signatures as an improvement of string-based signature-matching	–	attacks from Snort ruleset 23

Sr. No	Author	Year	Detection Technique	Datasets	Attack types
Vigna et.al. [109]	2003	Stateful intrusion detection	Snort	attacks from Snort ruleset	
24	P. Ning et.al. [110]	2003	pre-requisites and consequence model	Snort	attacks from Snort ruleset
25	S. Cheung et.al. [111]	2003	Alert correlation with multistep	DARPA	smurf, nmap, ipsweep, nmap , smurf, nmap, ipsweep, nmap
26	Kruegel et.al. [112]	2002	Stateful intrusion detection	NSL KDD	Probing, DoS, R2L, U2R
27	F. Cuppens et.al. [113]	2002	multi-step correlation algorithm	–	others
28	Julisch et.al. [114]	2002	Data mining with alarm clustering	Episode rules	others
29	Krishnamurthy et.al. [115]	2001	Stateful intrusion detection	–	others

2.8.3 Combined Approach

Vijaykumar, R. [33] will go through a crucial authentication phase that comprises login and password as well as e-mail, password, MAC address, password, and port number to analyse the signature. Anomaly-based detection will then commence depending on the speed 'r' threshold and bandwidth 'b' value. Few researchers combined few approaches together to build hybrid system , few are mentioned below in Table 2.6. Nave WEKA approaches, according to Hussein, S. M. [119], include Bayes, K-means, Bayes Net, WEKA, Snort, and Signature-based IDS. Bayes algorithms were used in this intrusion detection system.

A hybrid intrusion detection system, as described by Desai, A. S., et al. [120], detects both internal and external threats. Internal assaults are detected using a signature matching mechanism. External risks are identified using the Fuzzy genetic algorithm. To integrate ADS with SNORT, K. Hwang and colleagues [122] recommended using a weighted signature generation approach to extract signatures from observed abnormalities. HIDS takes signatures from the ADS output and adds them to SNORT's signature data storage to quickly and accurately identify the intrusion.

2.9 Algorithms

In order to satisfy the study's goals, assessed the applicability and efficiency of the following machine learning and deep learning methods. Machine learning and Deep learning methods such as Naive Bayes (NB), Support Vector Machine (SVM), Bayesian Network (BN), Voted Perceptron (VP), stochastic Gradient Descent (SGD),Random Forest, Deep neural network(DNN), Artificial Neural Network(ANN), Recurrent Neural Network (RNNs) etc.

2.9.1 Deep Neural Networks

The deep Neural Networks [27] [28] [30] [34] [40] [49] [50] [57] [59] [65] [73] [78] [93] is a multi-layered artificial neural neural network(ANN) compared to the rest of neural networks. First, to transform the input into the output, either linear or non-linear, the DNN discovers the right mathematical combinations. Then, by calculating probability movements across the layers the network models discover acceptable output.Figure 2.4 represents Deep neural network.

Table 2.6: Literature review of Combined Approach IDS

Sr. No.	Author Name	Year	Technique	Learning technique	Dataset	Attack type
1	K. Hwang et.al. [86]	2007	Machine learning	A SNORT and an anomaly detection subsystem (ADS) through automated signature generation from Internet episodes	MIT Lincoln Laboratories network traffic data	smurf, nmap, ipsweep, nmap , smurf, nmap, ipsweep, nmap
2	Ansam Khraisat, et.al. [117]	2020	Machine learning	C5.0 Decision Tree Classifier including One Support - Vector Machine	NSL-KDD and Australian Defence Force Academy (ADFA) Dataset	Probing, DoS, R2L, U2R
3	Kumar, R. [118]	2018	Machine learning	Login information like login and password and e-mail, password, MAC address, password, and port number. Then, based on the speed 'r' threshold and bandwidth 'b' value	Authentication steps	authentication

Sr. No.	Author Name	Year	Technique	Learning technique	Dataset	Attack type
4	Hussein, S. M. [118]	2016	Machine learning	Naïve WEKA methods include Bayes, K-means, Bayes Net with Snort	KDD Cup 99	Probing, DoS, R2L, U2R
5	Desai, A. S., et al. [120]	2016	Machine learning	Fuzzy Genetic algorithm used for Anomaly detection and signature matching used for SIDS	Snort ruleset	attacks from Snort ruleset
6	K. Hwang et al. [121]	2007	Machine learning	SNORT with ADS for a weighted signature generating method	MIT/LL attack data set	smurf, nmap, ipsweep, nmap , smurf, nmap, ipsweep, nmap

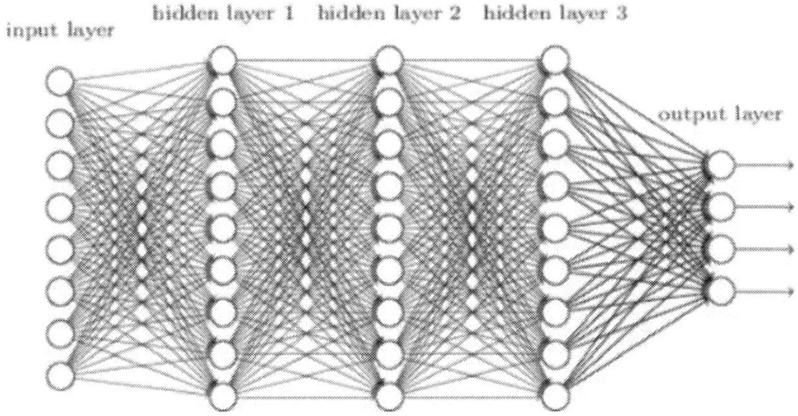

Figure 2.4: Deep Neural Network

2.9.2 Bayesian Network (BN) / Naive Bayes (NB)

BN [43] [52] [54] [74] [82] [100] [110] is a probabilistic technique that represents a collection of random variables and their conditional interactions using a directed acyclic graph. The NB classifier is built using a probabilistic approach. It's commonly assumed that variables are unaffected by the class or feature to which they've been allocated. Each class or characteristic is differentiated from the absence or occurrence of other traits by its existence. Depending on the specific structure of the probability model, supervised learning may be used to effectively train Naive Bayes classifiers. In a noisy setting, the NB classifier proved to be reliable. Rapid training (single scan), quick classification (non-sensitive to irrelevant characteristics), and it can handle both real and discrete data are all benefits of Naive Bayes.

2.9.3 Support Vector Machine (SVM)

SVM's [18] [51] [54] [55] [70] [74] [79] main premise is to increase sample dimensionality in order to separate them. The goal is to discover a hyperplane and fill it with samples from the same class. Linear boundaries in a bigger space, such as a polynomial, often result in more training class separation and translate to nonlinear boundaries in the original space. Because of its benefits, such as delivering extremely accurate classification findings, decreasing overfitting, and being noise resistant, SVM has been used in a number of recent IDS research. Nonetheless, it has limitations when compared to other classifiers, in that SVM is a binary classifier; however, pair-wise may be used to solve a multi-class classification issue (one class against all others, for all classes). SVM takes longer to execute since it is computationally intensive.

Figure 2.5 shows the block structure of an SVM classifier, with x representing the test set input vector and text i txi,i=1..., Ns representing the training set support vectors. Despite the fact that the block diagram topology of the SVM is similar to that of an RBF neural network, there are a few critical differences to be aware of: The RBF neural network's weights are set to minimise empirical error, while the SVM outputs' weights incorporate Lagrange multipliers (related with the constrained optimization in SVM learning that minimises the generalisation error). Second, although a typical multilayer neural network utilises activation functions to produce nonlinearity in the hidden layer, an SVM uses a kernel function k or nonlinearity in the hidden layer, and the kernel function is used in the hidden layer of an SVM.

2.9.4 Artificial Neural Network (ANN)

An artificial neural network [8] [48] [53] [57] [58] [84] [106] [119] [122] is a parallel distributed information processing model that is flexible (ANN). ANN is shown in Figure 2.6 Neurons (basic processing units), synapses (connections), network architecture (pattern of connectivity), and a learning method for training the network make up the network.

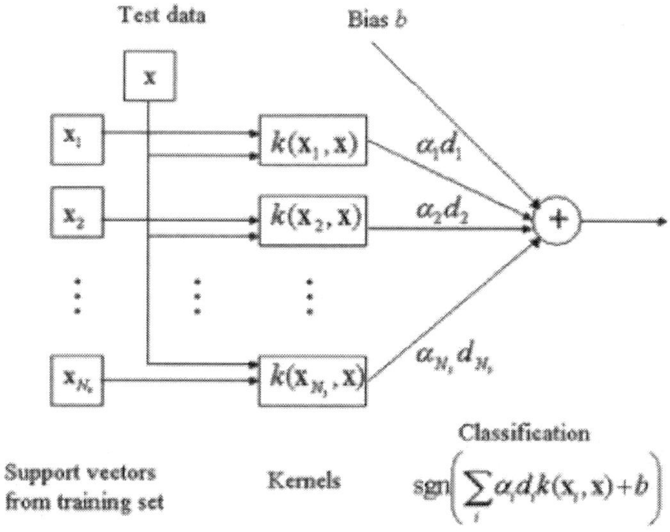

Figure 2.5: Support Vector Machine

The processing element is the most fundamental part of an ANN. They're in charge of all network computations on the local level. In most cases, multiplication, summation, and nonlinear mapping are utilised in the computations. Neurons are connected via synapses. Each link is a one-way connection that permits data to pass between two neurons.

The local biochemical environment of a link determines its strength and weakness, which is in turn influenced by the learning process' constant adjustment. There are two kinds of artificial neural networks: feedforward networks and recurrent networks. Learning is the process of determining if the connection pattern of a neural network is optimal or near to optimal. There are presently two kinds of learning algorithms: supervised (labelled) learning and unsupervised (unlabeled) learning.

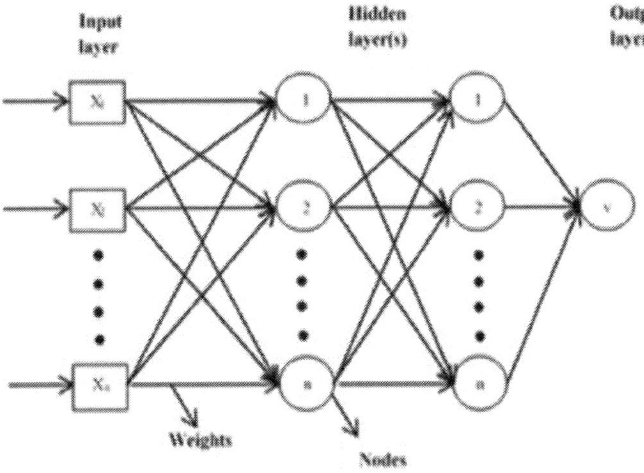

Figure 2.6: Artificial Neural Network

2.9.5 Deep Belief Networks (DBNs)

Deep Belief Networks (DBNs) [41] [55] [75] are stacked layers of Restricted Boltzmann Machines (RBM) that make up a Deep Neural Network. DBN can be used to solve unsupervised learning problems by reducing feature dimensionality, as well as supervised learning tasks such as classification and regression model development. Layer-by-layer training and fine-tuning are the two steps of DBN training. DBN is shown is Figure 2.7 Fine-tuning is the application of error back-propagation methods to fine-tune the parameters of DBN once the unsupervised training is completed [22]. Layer-by-layer training is the unsupervised training of each RBM, and fine-tuning is the application of error back-propagation methods to fine-tune the parameters of DBN once the unsupervised training is completed.

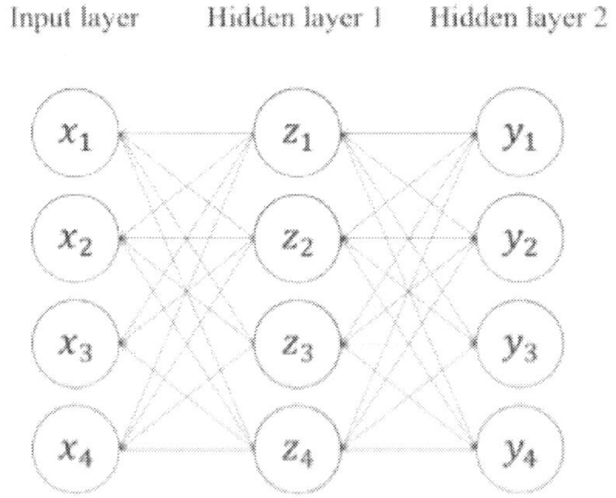

Figure 2.7: Deep Belief Networks

2.9.6 Recurrent Neural Network (RNNs)

A Recurrent Neural Network (RNN) [57] [67] [69] is a sort of artificial neural network in which nodes provide each other feedback signals. Hierarchical RNN, continuous-time RNN, bidirectional RNN, and the well-known Long Short-Term Memory (LSTM) network are all examples of designs that utilise this principle. RNNs have an internal memory that enables them to feel time in a natural way. RNN is shown in Figure 2.8 Traditional backpropagation methods, which need just feedforward connections between neurons, cannot be used to train these networks. The most common method is "backpropagation through time," which is a variation of this technique.

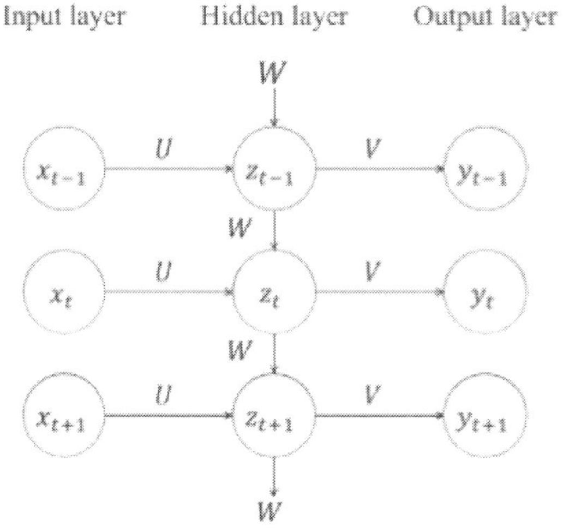

Figure 2.8: Recurrent Neural Network

2.9.7 Decision Tree (DT)

A decision tree [7] [56] [70] [74] [78] [80] [101] [105] [113] [122] [123][124] is a tree tree structure with each internal node representing an attribute test, each branch representing the test's conclusion, and each leaf node (terminal node) holding a class label. A tree may be "trained" by dividing the source set into subgroups based on attribute value tests. DT is shown in Figure

This approach is known as recursive partitioning because it is applied iteratively to each derived subset. The recursion is complete when all of the subsets at a node have the same value of the target variable, or when splitting no longer adds value to the predictions. A decision tree classifier may be built without any domain knowledge or parameter setting, making it ideal for exploratory knowledge discovery.

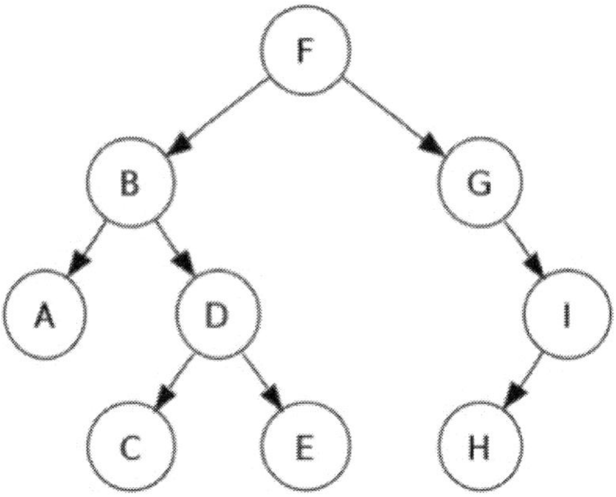

Figure 2.9: Decision Tree

2.9.8 Random Forest (RF)

In a tree induction process, RF [42] [48] [52] [95] uses an unpruned classification ensemble technique, transferring training data to bootstrap samples through random feature selection. RF is given is Figure 2.10. The final forecast is based on a majority vote for categorization of the ensemble's projections. Noisy data, as well as defects like the generalisation error rate, impeded it. The learning phase of RF was additionally impeded by high imbalance training datasets. The goal of RF is to reduce the overall degree of error rate by focusing more on the classifier's accuracy predictions on the popular class, which commonly influences the minority class, resulting in poor classification accuracy.

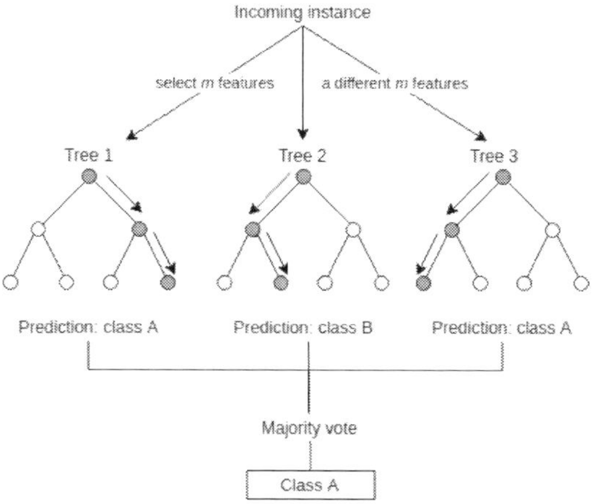

Figure 2.10: Random Forest

2.9.9 K-Nearest Neighbor

The Supervised Learning methodology is used in K-Nearest Neighbor[42], a fundamental Machine Learning method. The K-NN approach assumes that the new case/data and old cases are comparable and puts the new case in the most similar category to the existing categories. The K-NN algorithm keeps all of the current data and categorises incoming data points based on their similarities. This means that as new data is created, the K-NN approach can swiftly categorise it into a suitable category. Although the K-NN method may be used for both regression and classification, it is more typically employed for classification. K-NN is a non-parametric approach, meaning it doesn't make any assumptions about the data.

2.9.10 AdaBoost(AB)

AdaBoost[49] was one of the earliest boosting algorithms to be used in problem solving. Adaboost enables the combination of many ”weak classifiers” into a single ”strong classifier.” Here are some (interesting) statistics on Adaboost! In AdaBoost, decision stumps are weak learners. They are decision trees with a single split. AdaBoost works by providing more weight to situations that are difficult to categorise and less weight to situations that are already well-managed. AdaBoost's methods may be utilised to address classification and regression problems.

2.9.11 Convolution Neural Network (CNN)

A Convolutional Neural Network (ConvNet/CNN) [6] [18] [19] [20] [21] [28] [29] [31] [32] [33] [35] [41] [56] [61] [64] is a Deep Learning system that can take an input picture, assign relevance (learnable weights and biases) to various aspects/objects in the image, and distinguish between them. When compared to other classification methods, the amount of pre-processing required by a ConvNet is significantly less. While basic approaches need hand-engineering of filters, ConvNets can learn these filters/characteristics with enough training. The design of a ConvNet is inspired by the organisation of the Visual Cortex and is akin to the connection pattern of Neurons in the Human Brain. CNN is shown in Figure 2.11

Through the application of suitable filters, a ConvNet may successfully capture the Spatial and Temporal relationships in a picture. Due to the reduced number of parameters involved and the reusability of weights, the architecture performs superior fitting to the picture dataset. In other words, the network may be trained to better recognise the image's complexity.

2.10 Datasets for Intrusion Detection System

Datasets are playing very important role in designing IDS system. Selection of appropriate dataset is very crucial for any machine learning and deep learning algorithms.Table 2.7 gives papers categorise as per datasets, Figure 2.12 gives Survey based on Dataset and Table 2.8 gives Comparison of Dataset according to attacks. Few benchmark datasets are mentioned below.

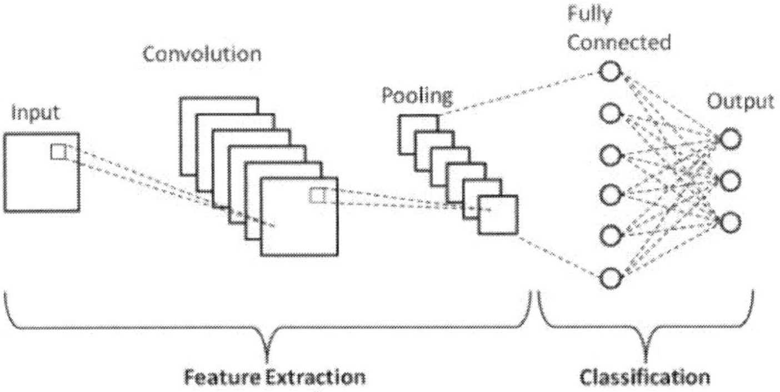

Figure 2.11: Convolution Neural Network

2.10.1 KDD 99 (University of California, Irvine 1998, 99)

The 1999 KDD Cup dataset was created from the 1998 DARPA tcpdump component processing. Advantage: KDD 99 includes more than 20 attacks such as Neptune-dos, pod-dos, smurf-dos, buffer overflow, rootkits, devil, teardrop and so on[1]. Advantages: Disadvantage: This data set was created when network traffic was combined in a simulated environment. The redundant records thus have a corruption that leads to biased test findings

2.10.2 DARPA (Lincoln Laboratory 1998, 1999)

For reasons of network security analysis, this dataset was generated. DARPA includes the sending and receipt of files via FTP, sending and receiving e-mails via SMTP and POP3, viewing websites, logging and operating on Telnet distant systems and the sending and receipt of IRC messages and remote router monitoring using SNMP[33]. Advantage: DOS, password devaluation, buffer overflow, remote FTP, sync, Nmaps and rootkit attacks. Inconvenience: for efficient IDS evaluation on modern networks, it is outdated in attack types and network architecture. It does not display the traffic in real networks, it contains anomalies such as the lack of false positives, and the IDS evaluation is out of date.

2.10.3 LIFE 3. (The Shmoo Group, 2000)

The 2000 DEFCON-8 dataset includes port scanners with buffer overflows, whereas the 2002 DEFCON-10 dataset uses port scanners and sweep scans, poor packets, administrator privilege protocol assaults and FTP. [34].

2.10.4 CAIDA (Applied Internet Data Analysis Center – 2002/2016)

CAIDA has three separate data sets: Most CAIDAs are highly accurate and anonymous with payload, protocol specifics and destinations for certain incidents or attacks. 1) CAIDA oC48 covering several types of data seen on the San Jose OC48 link supplied by members of the Caida, DARPA, NSF, DHS and Cisco;

2.10.5 CDX: CDX (United States Military Academy 2009)

The Dataset CDX shows how current data sets may be produced via network warfare competitions. Attackers were used to automatically conduct Nikto, Nessus and WebScarab samples and attacks in this dataset [33].

2.10.6 University of Kyoto - 2009 (University of Kyoto)

No manual labelling and anonymisation is available; however, the Network Traffic is limited since only attacks that can be detected on target honeypots. The dataset is made of honeypots. It provides a further 10 features for analyses and assessments of NIDS, including

IDS detection, malware detection and ashula detection, than before available [33].

2.10.7 20 (Twente University – 2009)

Three services, OpenSSH, Apache's web server and Proftp, using auth/ident on port 113, have been installed to set this dataset to the honeypot network[26].

2.10.8 UNSW NB 15

The UNSW-NB 15 dataset was created using raw network packets at the Australian Center for Cyber Security's (ACCS) Cyber Range Lab, leveraging the IXIA Perfect Storm platform to mix current normal operations with synthetic contemporary attack behavior[27].

2.10.9 CICIDS2017

The dataset now contains more recent and realistic statistics on binary assaults (PCAPs). It provides traffic analysis for the CICFlowMeter network, including flows with time stamps, source and destination IP addresses, source and destination ports, protocols, and assaults (CSV files).

2.10.10 NSL-KDD

NSL-KDD is a data set to overcome some of the issues inherent to KDD'99, as listed in [1][2][3]. In the NSL KDD data set, the assault classes are divided into four categories [5][9]: The following:

1. **DOS:** Service Denial is a kind of attack when it cannot deal with genuine demands by delivering numerous requests to the system, for instance, syn flooding. Relevant characteristics: 'source bytes' and 'percentage of error packages'
2. **Testing:** This attack monitors and monitors the remote target for information such as port scanning. Relevant characteristics: 'link duration' and 'source bytes'
3. **U2R:** This sort of attack is sometimes referred to as an unauthorised access to the root (local) privilege attack, by which a root/administrator attacker tries to obtain access to the root/ administrator rights by utilising a normal login account to the victim's system using for instance buffer overflow assault. Relevant characteristics: "file creation number" and "shell invocations number"
4. **R2L:** An attacker assaults a remote computer with local access to the victims' computer through a password deviating from

the distant computer with unregistered access. Important characteristics: Functions at network level – 'connection time,"service requested' feature, 'number of unsuccessful login attempts' host-level features.

Table 2.7: Papers categorise as per datasets

Sr. No.	Dataset	No. of Papers	Reference papers
1	KDD Cup 99	24	[6] [23] [31] [33] [34] [35] [39] [41] [42] [43] [44] [45] [48] [56] [59] [61] [62] [63] [74] [75] [77] [78] [70] [72]
2	NSL KDD	32	[1 – 4] [18] [19] [22] [24] [25] [28] [30] [32] [33] [36] [37] [40] [43] [45] [48] [49] [50] [51] [52] [58] [60] [63] [64] [63] [73] [76] [81]
3	UNSW 15	11	[1] [5] [8] [28] [29] [30] [34] [38] [57] [58] [60]
4	CICIDS 2017	7	[5] [7] [18] [21] [30] [38] [52]
5	DARPA	3	[20] [56] [69]
6	Kyto	2	[30] [43]
7	Snort	2	[44] [45]
8	Others	9	[3] [20] [30] [53] [56] [65] [83] [84]

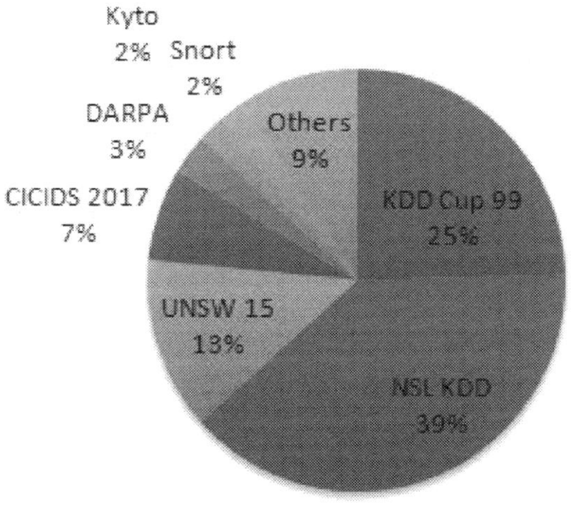

Figure 2.12: Survey based on Dataset

Table 2.8: Comparison of Dataset as per attack

Dataset	Browser Attack	Brute-force	DOS	SCAN	Back-door	DNS	Other
DARPA	Y	Y	Y	Y	N	N	Y
KDD99	Y	Y	Y	Y	N	N	Y
DEFCON	N	N	-	Y	N	N	Y
CAIDA	N	N	Y	Y	N	Y	Y
CDX	N	N	Y	Y	N	Y	–
Kyoto	N	Y	Y	Y	Y	Y	Y
Twente	N	Y	Y	Y	N	Y	Y
UNSW	N	N	-	Y	N	N	Y
CICIDS	Y	Y	Y	Y	Y	N	N
NSL KDD	Y	Y	Y	Y	Y	Y	Y

2.11 Research Gaps and Issues

- For predictive modelling, imbalanced classifications are a problem since most machine learning methods for classification were built with the assumption that each class had an equally large sample size. Models with low prediction accuracy, especially for minorities, are the outcome of this. Typically, the minority class has a greater impact on the issue, which makes it more vulnerable to categorization mistakes for the minority class than for the majority class. To solve this issue some researcher uses SMOTE[5][20].
- Anomaly-based IDS is commonly used to identify attacks because of deviations in the typical behaviour of malicious attackers from normal behaviour. In addition, because anomaly-based IDS doesn't require signatures to be previously saved, it may identify unknown threats but generate more false alarm [17][18][19] .
- While a range of security measures are employed to mitigate network security concerns, the likelihood of a networking device being compromised and falling into the hands of an attacker is quite high. There has been a lack of research attempting to uncover abnormalities in network behaviour when signature of attacks is not present in the dataset that may be linked to the networks' diverse and dynamic structure[90][91].

- IDS in use employ either anomaly- or signature-based detection techniques. Building an IDS by combining two approaches are challenging because of the complexity of the design[102].
- Existing IDS are "signature-based" because they look for a specific signature pattern and a specified pattern. These patterns make up the ruleset used by the IDS. Each packet is compared to a stored signature to identify infiltration. A ruleset-based IDS will identify an intrusion using a signature [103][104]. Signature-based IDS identifies attacks based on signatures, but it cannot identify unknown attacks since it doesn't analyse variations in behaviour.
- Few researcher combines this approaches, but none of them have adapted deep learning with updating signature into the rule set[105].

2.12 Conclusion

Recent IDS papers are reviewed and analyzed in this chapter. The study reveals the vast spectrum of IDS-building methods. Figure 2.2 depicts the most frequently used algorithms and their frequency of usage. In Table 2.4, each article's datasets and algorithms are listed.(i) Lack of datasets for intrusion detection on special-purpose networks like IoT and (ii) the dominance of Machine learning use to create anomaly-based IDS are two factors that restrict the availability and deployment of acceptable IDS. New deep learning approaches are required to create acceptable IDS that can learn from limited data and identify zero-day threats because of the speed at which new cyber assaults are popping up. A cyber threats taxonomy is used to highlight the gap. There are three categories in the taxonomy: active and passive threats, as well as those that are a combination of the two. Research gaps and issues are also given in this chapter.

3

Proposed System

3.1 Overview

Signature-based detection and anomaly-based detection are two methods of intrusion detection that are employed. An anomaly-based system is used to detect anomalous behaviour. Signature-based IDS employs rules to detect intrusions. Signature-based IDS scans signatures for attacks, however it is unable to detect unknown threats[14]. Anomaly-based IDS, on the other hand, may detect unknown assaults due to its enhanced examination of normal behaviour. The anomaly-based IDS detects unknown attacks by applying machine learning and deep learning techniques that use diverse methods. New types of attacks, including zero-day attacks, can be seen via anomaly-based methods. The proposed and implemented intelligent intrusion detection system in this dissertation will combine the advantage of Signature based detection and Anomaly-based detection techniques[15].

The results of the proposed systems meet the requirements of designing intrusion detection systems and maintaining high True Positive Rates and low False Positive Rates. This chapter proposes a novel intrusion detection system that includes Signature-based detection engine used for checking the attacks from the Signature Ruleset using Decision Tree and uses Deep learning algorithms to detect anomalies in the networks . This book provide a framework of the proposed system and discuss the intrusion detection process in detail. The combination of both detection system for detection of intrusion. Our findings show that the suggested intrusion detection system may efficiently detect real-world intrusions.

A proposed system is built using two layers of security. The first detection engine is signature-based detection, and the second detection engine is anomaly-based IDS. Proposed system architecture is given in the Figure 3.1, here details of modules are given. Detailed algorithm of full system is given in Algorithm 1.

- Step 1: Capture packet
- Step 2: Filter packet
- Step 3: Pre-processing of packet info
- Step 4: Detection Engine 1: Signature based IDS
- Step 5: Detection Engine 2: Anomaly based IDS
- Step 6: Create Signature and update Ruleset
- Step 7: Generate Alarm

3.2 Packet Capture

The data collecting process is a critical component of IDS's success. Packets are the units of data in the network. Tcpdump and Wireshark are two tools that may be used to capture packets from a network. Here used Python's Scapy to sniff HTTP packets on the network throughout this data collecting procedure. Here continue to sniff packets, and as they are received, this extract information from them [15], such as the source IP address, source port number, destination IP address,destination port, and so on. To analyse packets, this used the Python Scapy package because multiple network packets are supported, and classes are included to collect packets from various network segments and execute various actions with each one. It is shown in Module 1 how to retrieve packets from a network.

3.3 Filter Packet

The Scapy library's sniff function was deployed. This function is called anytime when new packet is received, and it is called with the filter parameter set to null because system is collecting all types of packets (tcp, ip, icmp) and the store parameter set to zero since system is only watching them.

3.4 Pre-processing of Packet Info

Characteristics like content and time-based features are included in data packets together with other properties like protocols, flags and other attributes like protocol type and operation. 1. Lable encoding: This dataset uses data encoding to transform the category values included in the features like duration(1), Flag(4),Service(3), Protocol type(2) and Label(42) to numerical values and 2. Data Normalization: Data normalisation is used to scale the feature values to a certain range. To access the Normalization function, this utilised Sklearn for pre-processing.

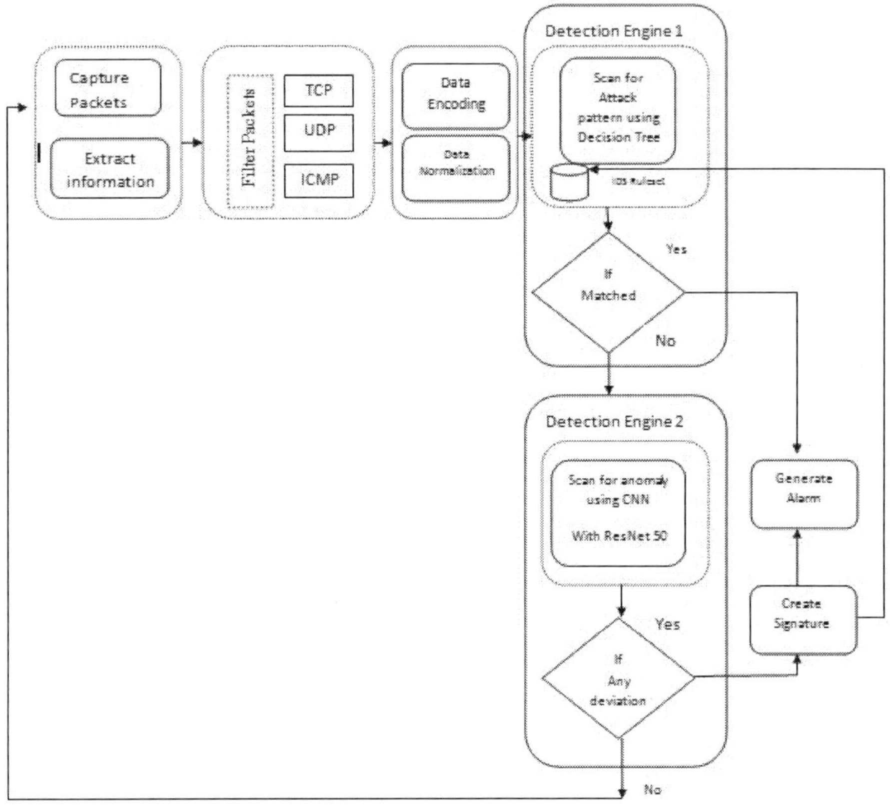

Figure 3.1: System Architecture

Algorithm 1: An algorithm of Full system

Data: *packets*

Result: *A*,N

1 For Intrusion detection System - Let be pattern vector:

ΣA = *Normal, AttackType*1, *AttackType*2, ..*or*ΣA = *N, A*1, *A*2, .., *An*

2 F, which is a feature set with a finite number of features. F= f1,f2......fn . Where, f1, f2, = the features. f1 is the duration; f2 is the protocol type (TCP, IP,UDP,ICMP, etc.), and f3 is the service that is being provided. The range (F) is denoted as f1*f2.....*fn. P=p1,p2,p3,...pn here P is live packet capture by IDS which contains different packets

3 S=Sig1,Sig2, Sig3. Sign where S for Signature rule set which contains various signature Sig1, Sig 2 and so on.

```
while p do
    if p1.sig ⊂ S then
        X ← A;
        Go to steps no. 22 ;
        break;
    else
        if p1.sig ⊄ S then
            if p1 is deviation from normal then
                X ← A;
                Create Signature and update into S R
                Go to steps no. 22 ;
                break;
            else
                end
                Output ← Normal;
                Go to step no 4 ;
            end
        end
        GenerateAlarm ;
    end
```

3.5 Signature based IDS

A Signature-Based method is used by most intrusion detection systems (IDS's) that correspond with preset signatures, which describe the harmful activity. The most resource-intensive IDS activity is the matching procedure[16]. Several systems achieve the correspondence between each input event and all rules. To enhance the matching process, a decision tree was presented that is created and adapted directly from the saved intrusion detection signatures. A decision tree is a network that resembles a tree and is made up of core nodes—attribute nodes—that act as tests for attributes, branch nodes—outcome nodes—that display the test results, and leaf nodes—class labels. The system determines the best route through the leaf nodes to go from the root node to the final destination. The dividing point is determined by the root node's most important characteristic. The details needed to assess the incoming data are included in the values and traits of each intermediary node in the tree. By moving through its internals from a root node to a leaf node, a tree that can anticipate additional information is constructed.Determining the value at which to divide the decision tree nodes presents a number of challenges [1,2,21]. Detailed explanation is given in Chapter No 4. The rules were split according to the three attributes starting from the source address and set in succession for the tree from left to right. The detection procedure begins at the tree base after the IDS has detected the rules for an input data item. Once the node obtains a label, system will look at the following feature. The attributes play's fundamental role is that it sets the stage for deciding which child node is to be selected[28]. The Ruleset is divided by the appropriate functionality, detection of a single child node must be maintained.

3.6 Anomaly based IDS

Anomaly-based detection creates a network traffic statistical model that reflects the typical baseline profile model, and then it identifies any behaviour that substantially deviates from it[36]. By looking for differences from the standard baseline model in the data being examined, anomaly detection attacks the issue and identifies new methods of attacks. However, since normal behaviour varies so considerably and it may be difficult to define typical behaviour in detail at times, this strategy can result in a considerable number of false alarms[37]. The novel approach sought to differentiate between deviant and typical user behaviour; if the observed behaviour deviated from the baseline profile, an alarm was issued to the system administrator. These detection systems, however, have significant drawbacks. For example, a poor detection rate for known attacks and a high false positive rate, which misclassifies regular network traffic as abnormal activity and sends an obnoxious alert to management.

The three primary types of deep learning algorithms are supervised, semi-supervised, and unsupervised [19]. When it comes to identifying intrusions, deep learning algorithms outperform traditional machine learning approaches. Convolutional neural networks exist in the world of deep neural networks [2]. Human feature extraction is required for knowledge acquisition, idea aspect analysis, and other machine learning approaches. 2D Convolutional layers in CNN reduce the time it takes to extract physical characteristics, making this CNN model more suitable for two-dimensional dataset processing.

As the number of layers grows, the accuracy is considered to get saturated. ResNet from Microsoft Research tackles the challenge of building deeper models with skip links (also known as shortcut connections or residuals). In our Intrusion Detection design, this used a Residual Network to solve the gradient vanishing/exploding issue.

Convolutional Neural Network with ResNet50, a 50-layer, is used in the model shown in figure 5.1. This method is more accurate and less prone to false alarms than typical machine learning techniques. All network packet information is categorised into two types: normal and attacks, which are used to detect network intrusions in the proposed IDS paradigm. The UNSW Canberra, Australia (UNSW2015) dataset , CICIDS2017 dataset,the NSL-KDD dataset from the Network Security Laboratory, are used to train and verify the proposed model. (UNSW). First, the ROC curve was used to assess and verify the model's precision, recall, F1 Score, accuracy. Its performance is then compared to other well-known machine learning classifiers, including Naive Bayes (NB), Support Vector Machine (SVM), k-Nearest Neighbor (kNN), Linear Regression (LR),Decision Tree (DT), AdaBoost (AB), Random Forest (RF). There is a 97.25% accuracy rate for the suggested model, which indicates that it has the potential to beat existing methods. Detailed explanation is given in Chapter No 5.

3.7 Create Signature and Update Ruleset

Extract the information from the packets and generate signature. Generated Signature, it follows the same signature as in SNORT rules. It automatically added into the ruleset. Detailed algorithm is given in the Algorithm 2.

Algorithm 2: An algorithm of Create signature and update ruleset

Data: *packets*

Result: *A*,N

while (NewPackets P1)

s1=generate signature(p1);

//here p1 is packet

add siganture into ruleset();

Output: alert udp 192.168.43.1 67 - 192.168.43.6 167 (msg: "Suspicious IP 192.168.43.1 and port 67 detected!"; reference: Anomaly; classtype:trojan-activity; sid:xxxx;

3.8 Generate Alarm

The OS module of python is used to call the system utility for generating sound in the system.

Algorithm 3: An algorithm of Generate alarm

Data: *packets*

Result: Attack-name,alarm

1 if A[index[length-1]]=='normal' or preds[0,index[length-1]]¡=0.60 :

2 print('—Mostly Predicted class:','normal')

3 else os.system('spd-say "Intrusion Detected" ')

4 print('—Mostly Predicted class:',A[index[length-1]],'— probabilities:', preds[0,index[length-1]],'—')

This Algorithm 3 shows generation of alarm when attack catches by system. This will generate alarm when probability of attack detection is more than 60 percent. So this will gives less no of false positives.

3.9 Conclusion

Using the well-known NSL KDD dataset, CICIDS 2017 dataset, and UNSW 2015 dataset, this research effort designs and develops an unique IDS technique by integrating Signature and Anomaly based IDS approaches. The given IDS has two detection engines: the first is based on a Decision Tree for signature-based IDS, and the second is based on the CNN ResNet 50 network for anomaly-based IDS, both of which are extremely valuable in cyber security research. Our proposed IDS, a three-stage learning process, develops signatures from the observed anomaly and has a high prediction accuracy at the classification method level, with a predictive accuracy of 98.98 percent. The suggested combined IDS based on the Decision Tree and CNN ResNet50 networks combines the strength of both Decision Tree and CNN ResNet50 networks, making it a viable solution. The hierarchical method of our IDS not only beats advanced IDS systems in terms of intrusion detection accuracy and false alarm reduction, but it also reduces false alerts. It's also put through its paces with real-time traffic from the local network.

4

Signature Based IDS

4.1 Introduction

A Signature-Based method is used by most Intrusion Detection Systems (IDS's) for detecting threats in the network using signature ruleset. The matching method is the most resource-intensive activity of an IDS following signature based techniques. Several systems achieve this matching by comparing each input event and all rules in the ruleset[12]. However, it's not even near to perfect. No general solution to this problem has yet been offered, despite ad-hoc optimizations at times. This book suggests a way to improve the matching process by utilising suitable algorithms. Signature based IDS (SIDS) is also known as Misuse detection[119]. Decision trees are faster to train and evaluate than random forests, since they require fewer computations.

Random forests require training multiple decision trees, which can be computationally expensive. So here considered decision tree for detecting threats.

Advantages of SIDS:

1. The mismatch detectors in SIDS module detect attacks without sending false alarms, which make them highly effective.
2. Specifically developed intrusion tools and technology can be immediately detected by Misuse detectors in SIDS module .
3. Misuse detectors offer system administrators an easy-to-use system monitoring tool even if they are not security experts.

Disadvantages of SIDS:

1. SIDS can only detect attacks that are previously known. Therefore, frequent updation of the signature of any discovered attack must be done in the ruleset.

2. The matching method is the most resource-intensive activity of an IDS following signature based techniques. Several systems achieve this matching by comparing each input event and all rules in the ruleset.
3. Despite the use of ad-hoc optimisations, no general solution has yet been developed.

Motivation of using Decision Tree in SIDS Detection Engine:

A signature-based approach is used by majority of intrusion detection systems, where attacks are identified by comparing each input event against previously created signatures that identifies malicious behaviour, which is most resource-intensive task. Majorly systems carry out the above mentioned task by progressively applying each input event to each rule. So to avoid this, decision tree is used to identify malicious events owing to its architectural design as it dictates the criteria for matching at every node. This will reduce the redundant comparisons.

4.2 System Architecture of SIDS Detection Engine

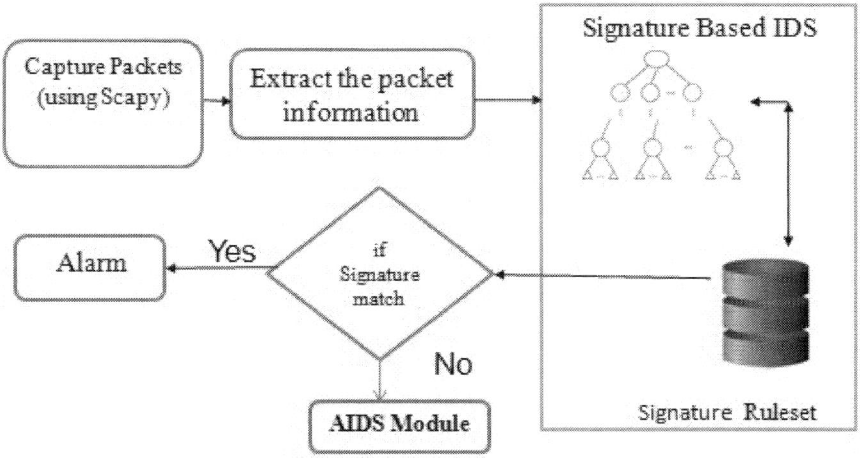

Figure 4.1: Signature based IDS Detection Engine 1

Figure 4.1 depicts SIDS module involving packet capture, extraction of information from packets like source address , destination address, port no etc., further utilizing the packet information to find the type of attack using appropriate method like decision tree which is formed from signature based ruleset. A decision tree containing a number of signatures, is used to discover hazardous events with as few repeating comparisons as possible. SIDS examine system actions and try to match these actions with known attacks , which already have system definitions or signatures in the ruleset [1,2,21] .

4.2.1 Packet Capture

The data collecting process is a critical component of IDS's success. Packets are the units of data in the network. Tcpdump and Wireshark are two tools that may be used to capture packets from a network. Here used Python's Scapy to sniff HTTP packets on the network throughout this data collecting procedure. Here continue to sniff packets, and as they are received, system extract information from them [23], such as the source IP address, source port number, destination IP address,destination port , and so on. To analyse packets, system used the Python Scapy package because multiple network packets are supported, and classes are included to collect packets from various network segments and execute various actions with each one. .

4.2.2 Extract the information from packets

The Scapy library's sniff function was deployed. This function is called anytime when new packet is received, and it is called with the filter parameter set to null because system is collecting all types of packets (tcp, ip, icmp) and the store parameter set to zero since System are only watching them.

Sniffing Result : [IP HEADER]

version : 4

IHL: 20 bytes

Tos:40

Total Length :52

Identification : 4983

Flags : DF

Fragment Offset : 0

TTL: 56

Protocol: 6

Header checksum : 19177

Source : 49.44.198.218

Destination : 192.168.43.141

Source Port : 80 Destination Port: 53390

Sequence Number: 1756565665

Acknowledgment Number : 912356495

Data Offset : 8

Flags : A

Window Size : 260

Checksum : 51126

Options: (timestamp(1392071508))

4.3 Mapping of Rules with features of NSL KDD dataset

Table 4.1: Mapping of Rules with features of NSL KDD dataset

Attribute Name	Rule Keyword	Short Description
ip_proto	Protocol	IP protocol type
src_ip	Source IP address	Source IP address
dst_ip	DestinationIP address	Destination IP address
service	Destination port no	Service type . e.g. http
icmp_type	Itype	ICMP message type
src_bytes	DSize	Packet Payload size
flags	Flags	TCP flags
land	Sameip	Source and destination addresses are the same
Src_count	threshold:track by_src$_c$*ount*	No of connections to the same destination
Dst_count	threshold:track by_dst$_c$*ount*	No of connections to the same source

Features of Snort dataset and NSL KDD dataset are mapped as shown in Table 4.1 to create dataset which will be used to the test the result when Signature-based and Anomaly-based IDS are combined.

4.4 Dataset Prepared from the Snort Rule

Table 4.2: Sample dataset from Snort IDS

Protocol	SourceIP	Src portno	DestIP	Dest port no	flow	content	Class type	Message
tcp	$ HOME$_N ET$	513	$ EXTERNAL _NET	any	to _ client, established	login incorrect, fast_ pattern, nocase	unsuccessful -user	PROTOCOL -SERVICES rlogin login failure
tcp	$ HOME$_N ET$	513	$ EXTERNAL _NET	any	to _ client, established	—01—r logind—3A— Permission denied.,fast _pattern,nocase	unsuccessful -user	PROTOCOL -SERVICES r login login failure
tcp	$ HOME$_N ET$	666	$ EXTERNAL _NET	any	to _client, established	FTP Port open	misc-activity	MALWARE BACKDOOR BackConstruction 2.1 Server FTP Open Reply

Protocol	SourceIP	Src portno	DestIP	Dest port no	flow	content	Class type	message
tcp	\$ HOME$_N ET$	2401	\$ EXTERNAL _ NET	any	to _ client, established	E protocol error—3A— Root request missing,fast _ pattern,nocase	misc-attack	INDICATOR -COMPROMISE CVS missing cvsroot response
tcp	\$ HOME$_N ET$	2589	\$ EXTERNAL _NET	any	to _ client, established	2—00 00 00 06 00 00 00—Drives—24 00—,depth 16	misc-activity	MALWARE -BACKDOOR - Dagger$_1$.4.0

Dataset is prepared from the snort rule where mapping between packets information and Snort rules is performed. Table 4.2 includes the sample dataset from Snort IDS.

4.4.1 Formation of Decision Tree

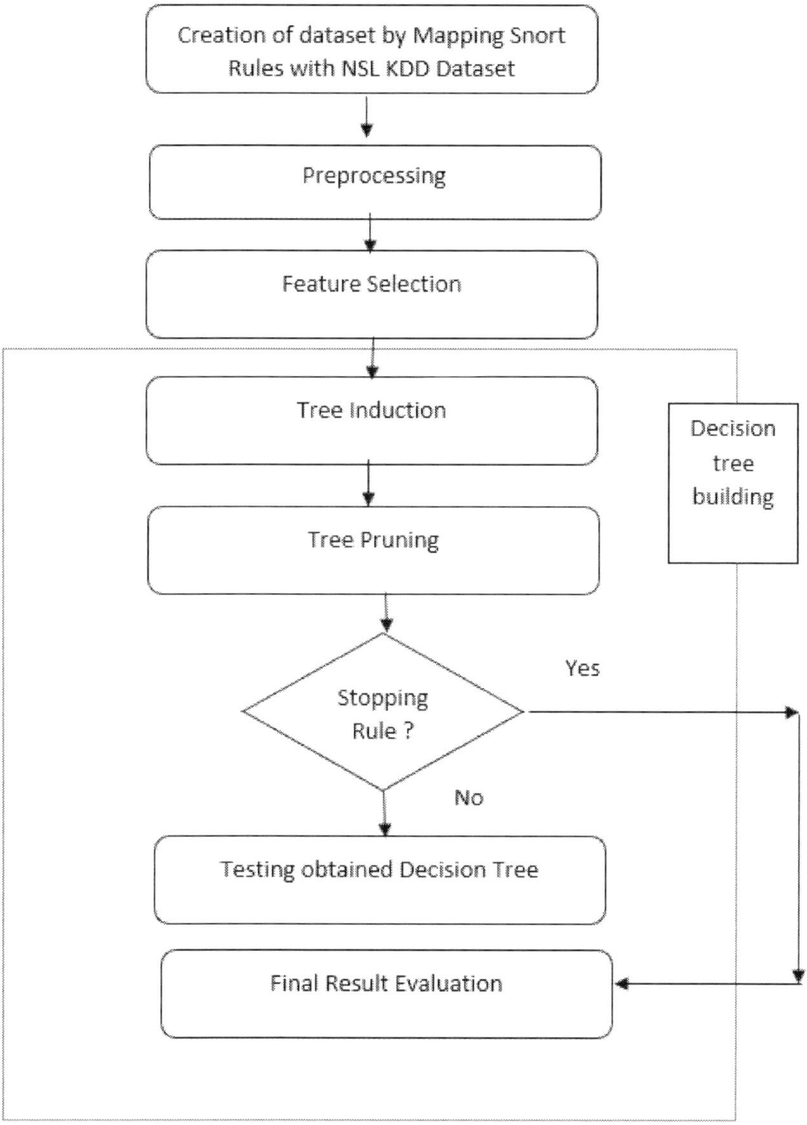

Figure 4.2: Steps to build Decision Tree

Steps to build decision tree is shown in Figure 4.2. Each input event used by SIDS is compared to established signatures of attack behaviour using the signature approach. The IDS job that uses the greatest resources is the matching approach. The majority of systems progressively check each input event with all rules until the first attack is discovered. To enhance the matching process, a decision tree was presented that is created and adapted directly from the saved intrusion detection signatures. For supervised classification learning and regression, decision trees are a non-parametric and non-linear data mining technique. The system determines the best route through the leaf nodes to go from the root node to the final destination. The dataset for the first phase is chosen from the NSL-KDD dataset repository map this with Snort Rules. Then, preprocessing is used on a set of data to change a non-numeric property to a numeric one. The next three phases includeed while building decision tree, which comprise tree induction, tree pruning, and evaluating the resulting tree with a test dataset, . Recursive partitioning technique (CART) [29] builds binary decision trees by slicing them at each node. The decision tree's root node includes complete training samples. The last phase involves evaluating performance using a variety of performance metrics, including classification accuracy, F1 Score, precision and recall. In the Tree induction decrease in impurity for each potential split of an individual attribute during the tree induction phase since each and every connection pattern in this situation comprises discrete and continuous valued attributes. The dataset is given its own decision tree, one for each of the five classes (normal and types of attack) To prevent data over-fitting, the generated decision tree is pruned. Outliers and noise in the dataset cause over-fitting to happen. The suggested solution employs post pruning, which uses error rate (pattern misclassified by tree) as the pruning criterion, to solve this issue. After each stage of trimming, the tree is tested to determine the results.

The dividing point is determined by the root node's most important characteristic. The details needed to assess the incoming data are included in the values and traits of each intermediary node in the tree. By moving through its internals from a root node to a leaf node, a tree that can anticipate additional information is constructed. Determining the value at which to divide the decision tree nodes presents a number of challenges.

By analysing characteristics, a decision tree may detect potentially risky network behaviours. This system may be used to assess the security of multiple intrusion detection systems in an enormous data collection of intrusion occurrences. Attack signatures and other monitoring operations can continue while trends and patterns are growing. Decision trees are superior to different categorisation approaches because they allow various rules, which are readily understandable and feasible with applications in real-time. Until a basic decision tree is utilised, all rules may be speedily identified with the lowest number of comparison elements. For the creation of subgroups, a decision tree is beneficial; the result of rules is split. This form enables us to locate the tree's root node, which constitutes all rules. The subsets that the children of the tree form are equal to the subsets obtained by dividing the set rule by the first property. Each branch in the tree has a subgroup attached to it[30]. If a node has several rules, then the rules are separated, and the division's features are given a single name. This feature is annotated with an arrow that leads from a child to a parent, and all of the rules on that child node include the value of the feature in parentheses. There are only a few unique rules for each leaf node in the tree and no distinctive features. Regulations are indistinguishably evident if all the features are the same in the clustering process. This is followed by an example where four rules and three characteristics are taken into account. A rule defines the properties of network packets coming from a given source address to a defined destination and port. While IPv4 source and destination port are used for the destination integer port, IPv4 type of source and destination is used for the source integer port.

This uses a signature method where each input event is compared to known patterns of risky behaviour. The IDS job that uses the greatest resources is the matching approach. Finally, a lot of systems compare each input event against each rule.

(#) Source Address – → *DestinationAddress* : *DestinationPort*

(1) 172.16.1.1 – → 172.16.1.2 : 23

(2) 172.16.1.1 – → 172.16.1.3 : 23

(3) 172.16.1.1 – → 172.16.1.3 : 25

(4) 172.16.1.4 – → 172.16.1.5 : 80

A possible decision tree in the case discussed above is shown in Figure 4.3. The rules were split according to the three attributes starting from the source address and set in succession for the tree from left to right. The detection procedure begins at the tree base after the IDS has detected the rules for an input data item. Once the node obtains a label, system will look at the following feature. The attributes play's fundamental role is that it sets the stage for deciding which child node is to be selected. The Ruleset is divided by the appropriate functionality, detection of a single child node must be maintained.

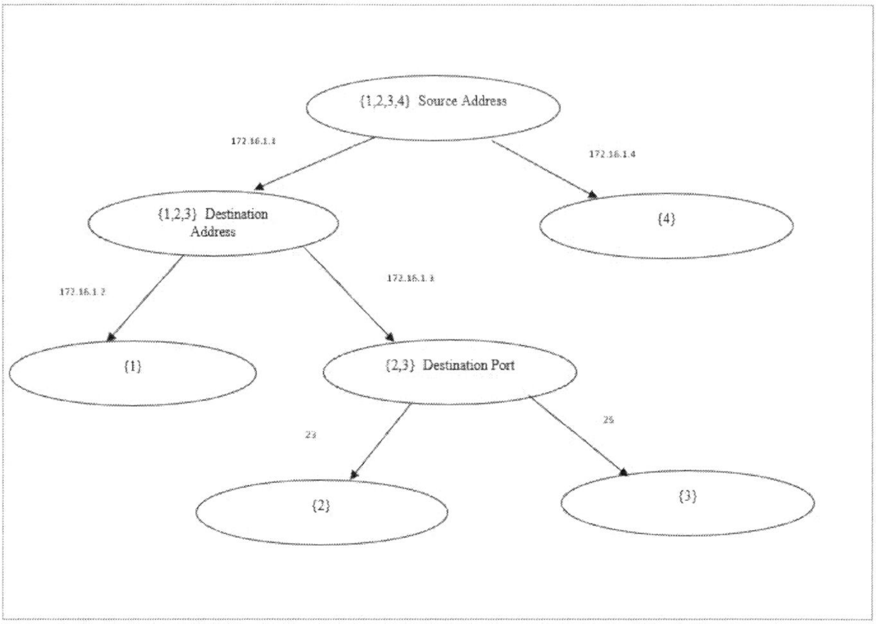

Figure 4.3: Decision tree from packet data

All rules relevant to the node are presented in the leaf node. Additional functions may be required even if these other features are implemented. There has not previously been a partition of the features on the route to this leaf, to this stretch of the road must be reassessed. The root node is linked to a target port and the source and destination addresses, but the two are not applied to the target port. The rule determination procedure will ultimately reach the leaf node holding Rule 1 while processing an input packet transmitted from 172.16.1.1 to 172.16.1.5. However, the rules may need to be modified because the packet might have been transferred to another port. The destination port must thus be double-checked. If unique characteristics are not specified, they are just added to the tree. Thus, need to do to divide a node is to 'partition' the node, leading to only one child node. If the detection technique cannot discover a successor node with a matching rule, there is no matching rule. This helps to exit the matching procedure by returning as fast as feasible. Decision tree is formed using 10 rules are given as sample in Figure 4.3. Every step in the decision tree from beginning to end must be completed. Developing the tree entails implementing a feature selection on each group of rules (i.e., partitioning the corresponding rules). This method is not used if there is no rule to recognise a feature. As with having one node with the same set of rules, it would just be the same thing. This second component ensures that every node in the tree from the root down clears any partitioning characteristics previously utilised.

4.4.2 Building and working of Decision Tree

The proposed system employs the correlation-based feature selection (CFS) technique to reduce dimensionality and the CART algorithm with the gini index as splitting criteria for pattern classification. Utilizing distinct testing data from the benchmark NSL-KDD dataset, the suggested approach has been evaluated. The accuracy is increased by the feature selection approach. Sample Decision tree generated from the dataset is shown in Figure 4.4. Gini's impurity index is used as the splitting criteria in the classification method Classification And Regression Trees (CART) [1] for creating decision trees. CART is a binary tree that is created by repeatedly dividing a node into two child nodes[117].

Mathematical Model of Decision Tree

This algorithm first builds a decision tree using the BuildTree function, which takes in a set of training data D, a splitting criterion C, and a maximum depth m. The resulting tree is then used to classify new instances using the Classify function, which takes in the decision tree T and the instance to classify x. The algorithm recursively traverses the decision tree, following the appropriate edges based on the attribute values of the instance, until it reaches a leaf node with a class label. The class label is then returned as the classification result. Let X be the input feature vector and y be the target variable. Let T be a decision tree consisting of internal nodes, leaf nodes, and edges. Each internal node i of the tree is associated with a feature $f(i)$ and a threshold $t(i)$. The decision tree recursively splits the data into subsets based on the values of the features. At each internal node, the data is split into two subsets based on the value of the associated feature:

The left child of the node corresponds to the case where $f(i) \leq t(i)$. The right child of the node corresponds to the case where $f(i) > t(i)$. The tree is built by recursively repeating the above step until the data subsets at the leaf nodes are pure or until a stopping criterion is met. The output of the decision tree for a given input X is the class or predicted value associated with the leaf node reached by following the decision path through the tree based on the values of the input features.

Algorithm 4: An algorithm of building and working of Decision tree

```
Require: Training data D, Splitting criterion C, Maximum depth m
function BUILDTREE(D, C, m)
    Create a new tree node N
    if All instances in D belong to the same class then
        Label N as a leaf node with the class label
    else if The depth of N is greater than or equal to m then
        Label N as a leaf node with the majority class label in D
    else
        Choose the best attribute A to split D based on C
        Label N with A
        for Each possible value v_i of A do
            Let D_i be the subset of instances in D where A = v_i
            if D_i is empty then
                Create a new leaf node with the majority class label in D
                Add the leaf node as a child of N with edge labeled as v_i
            else
                Create a new child node of N with edge labeled as v_i
                Set the child node to be the result of calling BUILDTREE(D_i, C, m)
            end if
        end for
    end if
    return N
end function
Require: Decision tree T, Instance to classify x
function CLASSIFY(T, x)
    if T is a leaf node then
        return the class label of T
    end if
    Let A be the attribute label of T
    Let v be the attribute value of x for A
    Let T' be the child node of T with edge labeled as v
    return the result of calling CLASSIFY(T', x)
end function
```

Note that there are many variations of decision tree algorithms that use different splitting criteria and pruning techniques.

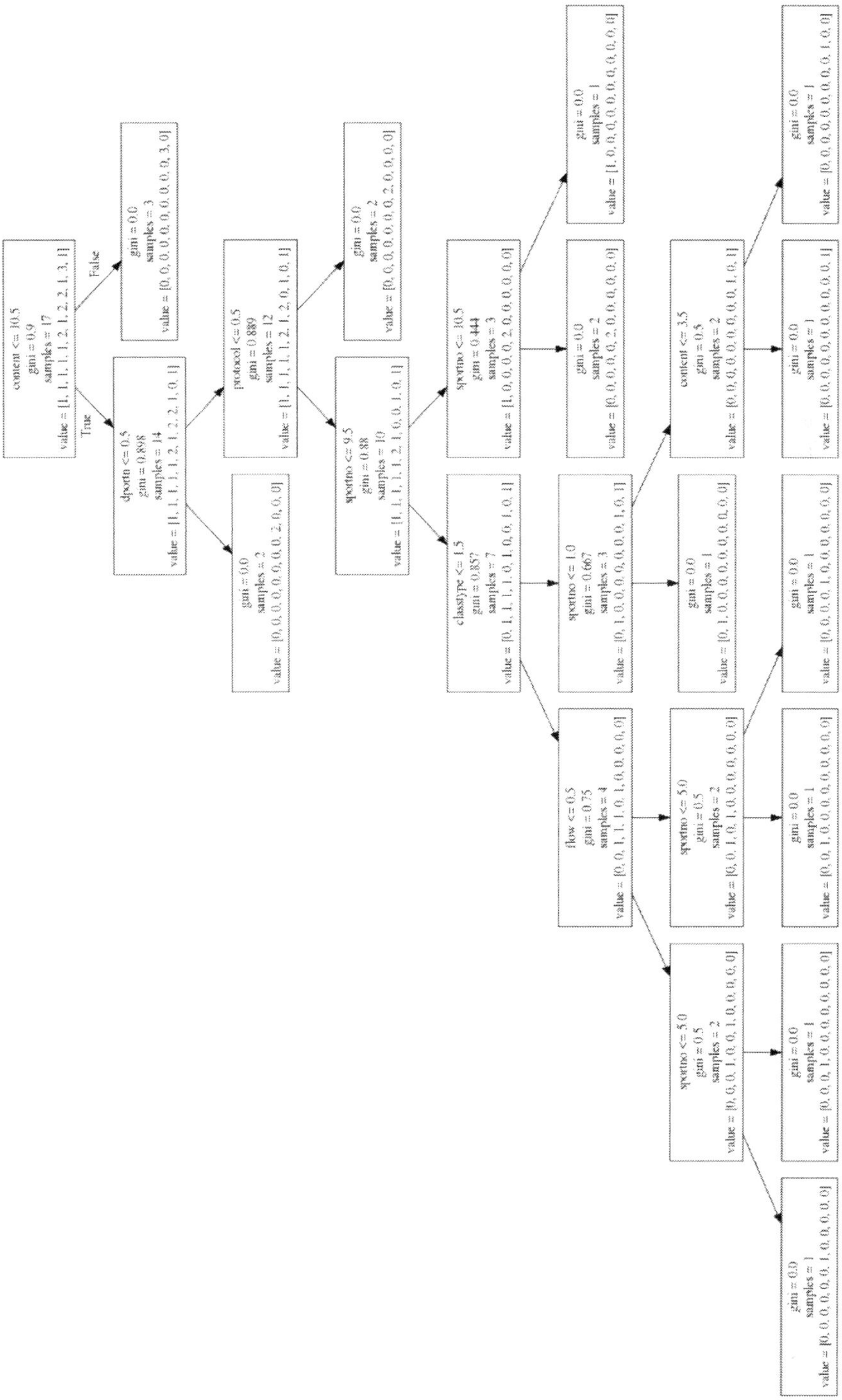

Figure 4.4: Generated Decision Tree

4.5 Generate Alarm

The OS module of python is used to call the system utility for generating sound in the system. When signature matches in the decision tree then alarm is generated otherwise request goes to AIDS Module. Details are given in section 3.8.

4.5.1 Result and Discussion

The SIDS is largely based on a Decision Tree for signature-based Intrusions, which are highly useful in cybersecurity research because to their 96.96 percent accuracy. Also if the Signature based detection engine not able to detect the intrusion then control goes to anomaly based detection engine.

Table 4.3: Signature Based Intrusion Detection System

Sr. No.	Evaluation Parameters	Percentage
1	Precision	96%
2	F1- Score	95%
3	Accuracy	96.96%
4	Recall	95%

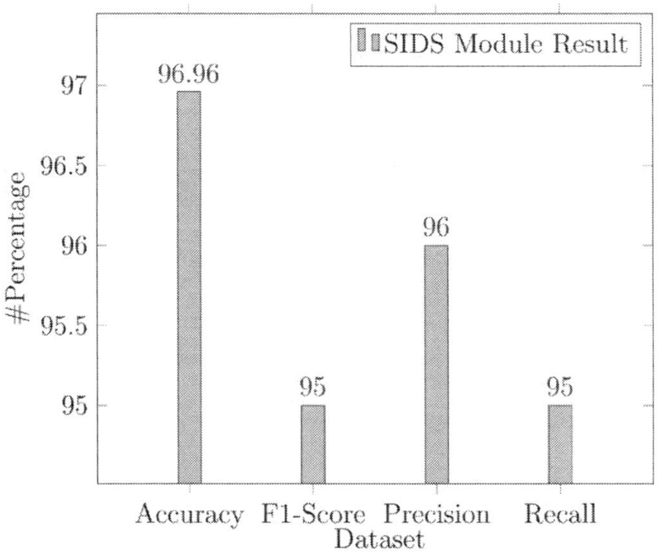

Figure 4.5: SIDS Module Result

Result of SIDS detection engine is given below in Table 4.3 and Figure 4.5. Proposed SIDS detection engine gives accuracy of 96.96%.

4.6 Conclusion

For the majority of IDS, a signature method is used, in which each input event is evaluated against current signatures of attack behaviour. The IDS job that requires the greatest resources is the matching approach. Many systems eventually compare each input event to each rule. The IDS offered is mostly based on a Decision Tree for signature-based IDS, which are very beneficial in cybersecurity research owing to their 96.96 percent accuracy. Anomaly-based detection engines take over if the signature-based detection engines fail to find the incursion.

5

Anomaly Based IDS

Introduction

Anomaly-based detection creates a statistical model of normal network traffic that describes the expected baseline profile and then recognises any behaviour that deviates considerably from it[115]. Anomaly detection addresses the issue by looking for deviations from the standard baseline model in the data under study. While this enables anomaly to detect novel forms of assault, it can result in a significant number of false alarms due to the fact that normal behaviour varies widely and is frequently difficult to fully describe. The anomalous technique attempted to distinguish between abnormal activity and user behaviour; an alert was generated for the system administrator if observed behaviour deviated from the baseline profile. However, these detection methods continue to have serious flaws. For example, a low detection rate for known assaults and a high false positive rate misclassify typical network traffic as abnormal activity, generating an obnoxious warning to the management[116].

The suggested intrusion detection system is composed of four critical components, as seen in Figure 5.1.

1. **Packet Capturing module:** Using packet sniffing tools, collects packets.
2. **Data pre-processing:** Data encoding, data normalisation, and data balancing are all included in pre-processing.
3. **Intrusion Detection Engine:** This engine detects attacks by using a CNN-based ResNet architecture.
4. **Output/Report module:** Generate an alert in response to detecting an intruder.

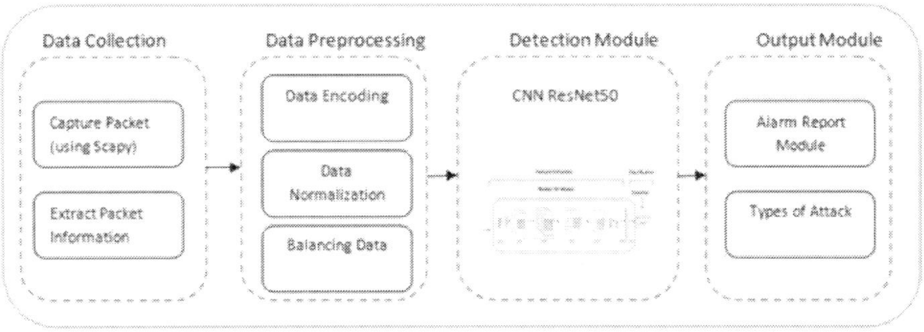

Figure 5.1: Anomaly Based IDS System Architecture

5.2 Data Collection

The manner of data collection is crucial to IDS's success. Packets are used to transport data across the network. Several programmes, such as tcpdump and Wireshark, are available for gathering packets from a network. Using Python's Scapy, this gathered data by sniffing HTTP packets on the network. It continues to sniff packets and get information such as the source port number, source IP address, and destination IP address. It selected the Python Scapy module to analyse packets because it supports a variety of network packets, offers classes for packet capture from network segments, and invokes a function whenever a new packet is recorded[116].

Algorithm 4: An algorithm of Packet capture

```
from threading import Thread
from scapy.all import *
define inPacket(self, pkt)
define stopfilter(self, x)
define run(self):
print("Sniffing started.")
sniff(prn=self.inPacket, filter="", store=0, stop filter=self.stopfilter)
```

Utilizing the sniff function from the Scapy library is Algorithm 5 above. The prn parameter calls inPacket(self,pkt) when a new packet arrives, with the filter parameter set to null to capture all packet types, including tcp, ip, and icmp, the store parameter set to 0 to indicate that this is only monitoring packets and not storing them, and the stop filter set to stop the thread from running.

5.3 Dataset - Dataset pre-processing

5.3.1 Dataset Information

For effective model training, it is critical to choose a suitable dataset with the most important attributes and attack types [15]. Three important datasets is shown in Table 5.1 considered in system to evaluate the system. Datasets information is given in Table 5.2 which includes attack information. Comparison of datasets presented using graph in Figure 5.2, here Figure

5.2.a indicates no. of records as per dataset, Figure 5.2.b indicates no. of features per dataset and Figure 5.2.c indicates no. of attacks per dataset. It is observed that UNSW15 contains more records of data as compared with other two datasets. CICIDS2017 dataset includes more no of attacks and features as compared with other two datasets.

Table 5.1: Dataset information

Dataset	Records	Features	Attack Categories	Reference papers
UNSWNB15	257673	47+2	9	[1] [5] [8] [20] [21] [22] [26] [30] [49] [50] [52]
CICIDS2017	2830751	83+1	14	[5] [7] [9] [13] [22] [30] [44]
NSLKDD	148517	41+2	4	[14] [10] [11] [14] [16] [17] [20] [22] [24] [25] [28] [29] [32] [35] [37] [40] [41] [42] [43] [44] [50] [52] [55] [56] [58] [65] [68] [73]

Many scholars regard the NSL KDD dataset to be a benchmark dataset in their study. It outperforms the KDD 99 dataset because there are no duplicate records in the test set, resulting in a higher reduction rate. UNSD – NB 15, which contains the most recent assault data, is another benchmark dataset. The Canadian Institute for Cybersecurity issued the CICIDS2017 dataset in 2017, which included benign and up-to-date attack information. Three datasets were used in the experiment, each with a different amount of records, characteristics, and attack types addressed.

Table 5.2: Dataset with attack information

Year	Dataset	Normal	DOS	DDOS	Probe	U2R	R2L	Worms	SSH	FTP	Backdoor	Brute Force	XSS	SQL Injection	Shell Code	Fuzzer	Botnet	PortScan	Exploits
2017	CICIDS 2017	Y	Y	Y	-	-	-	-	Y	Y	-	Y	Y	Y	-	-	Y	Y	-
2017	UNSW NB 2015	Y	Y	-	-	-	-	Y	-	-	Y	-	-	-	Y	Y	-	-	Y
2000	NSL KDD	Y	Y	-	Y	Y	Y	-	-	-	-	-	-	-	-	-	-	-	-

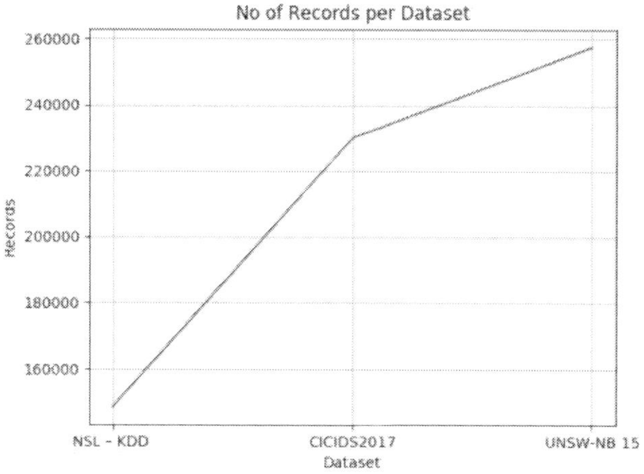

(a) No. of records per dataset

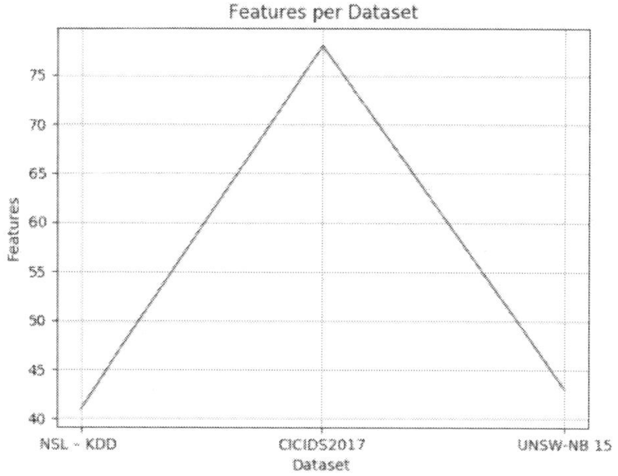

(b) No. of features per dataset

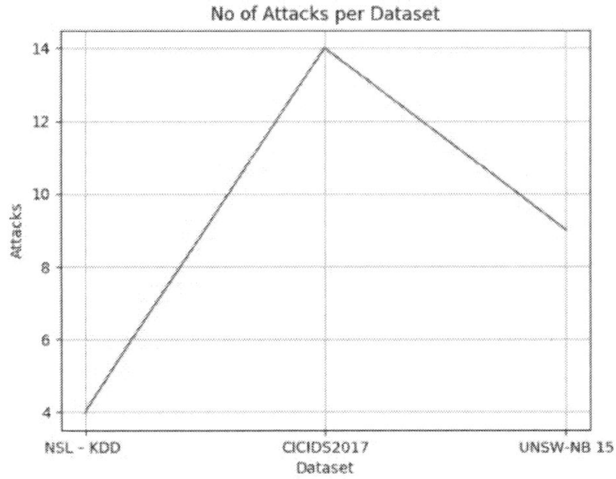

(c) No. of attacks per dataset

Figure 5.2: Graphs of Comparison of Dataset

NSL-KDD

The benchmark utilised by intrusion detection systems, the NSL-KDD dataset from the University of New Brunswick is an updated version of the KDD'99 dataset. There are 43 functions per dataset entry. The remaining two (normal/attack and traffic input severity signals) are category labels, leaving 42 of them to be traffic entry characteristics. Each record in a data collection contains 43 attributes, as shown in Table 5.3. Attributes including intrinsic, content, host-based, and time-based properties are included in Table 5.4. Information on attacks on the NSL KDD dataset is included in Table 5.5.

Table 5.3: NSL KDD Dataset features.

Sr.No.	Name of the feature	Sr.No.	Name of the feature
1	Dur	22	Cnt
2	Proto_ type	23	Srv_cnt
3	Service	24	Serror_cnt
4	Flg	25	Srv_error_rate
5	Source_byts	26	Rerror_rate
6	Destination_byts	27	Srv_rerror_rate

Sr.No.	Name of the feature	Sr.No.	Name of the feature
7	Land	28	Sae_srv_rate
8	Wrong_fragments	29	Dif_srv_rate
9	Urgent	30	Srv_diff_host_rate
10	Hot	31	Dst_host_rate
11	No_of_failed_logins	32	Dst_host_cnt
12	Logged_in	33	Dst_host_srv_cnt
13	No_compromised	34	Dst_host_same_srv_rate
14	Root_shell	35	Dst_host_same_src_port_rate
15	Su_attempted	36	Dst_host_same_diff_host_rate
16	No_file_creations	37	Dst_host_same_diff_host_rate
17	No_shells	38	Dst_host_serror_rate
18	No_access_files	39	Dst_host_srv_rerr_rate
19	No_outbound_cmds	40	Dst_host_rerr_rate
20	Is_host_login	41	Dst_host_rerr_rate
21	Is_guest_login	42	Class_label

The most of them include information on traffic input analysis (e.g). It contains information such as the number of connections attempted to the same host in a two-second interval.

Table 5.4: NSL KDD Dataset categories of features

Sr.No.	Types of Features	Features	Remarks
1	Content features	10-22	This information comprises information about the original packets since the packets are transmitted in many pieces rather than one.
2	Intrinsic features	1–9	This field contains the packet's fundamental information.

Sr.No.	Types of Features	Features	Remarks
3	Host-based features	23-31	The most of them include information on traffic input analysis (e.g). It contains information such as the number of connections attempted to the same host in a two-second interval.

Table 5.5 displays intrusion data from the NSL KDD dataset. The four forms of attacks are User to Root, Denial of Service (DoS), Probe (U2R), and Remote to Local (R2L).

Table 5.5: NSL KDD Dataset Attack information

Attack Types	Attack Names	Remarks
Probe	Ipsweep, portsweep, mscan,saint	A probe or surveillance attack attempts to get data over the network.
Denial of Service (DoS)	satan,apache2, udpstorm, back, land, smurf,mailbomb, Neptune, udpstorm, pod, processtable, teardrop	Traffic flow to and from the principal system is disrupted by a denial-of-service (DoS) attack.
Remote to Local (R2L)	xsnoop, ftp_write, phf, guess_passwd, imap,named, multihop, sendmail, snmpguess snmpgetattack, xlock , spy, warezclient, worm , warezmaster	An intrusion that attempts to get local access to a distant workstation is known as Remote to Local.

Attack Types	Attack Names	Remarks
User to Root(U2R)	Loadmodule, buffer_overflow, perl, xterm, httptunnel, rootkit , ps, sqlattack,	The U2R attack aims to get access to the system or network (root), starting with a normal user account and progressing to super-user status.

CICIDS2017 Dataset

Data sets must be updated to represent current attack patterns, however, since attack techniques are always developing. The CICIDS2017 Dataset was also utilised to train the model as a benchmark dataset. This information is organised into eight comma-separated value files, each including five days of network activity. Table 5.6 gives the features of CICIDS dataset, Table 5.7 gives details of attacks associated with dataset.

Table 5.6: CICIDS dataset Features

Feature No.	Name of the feature	Feature No.	Name of the feature	Feature No.	Name of Feature
1	FlowId	29	Fwd IATMax	57	Down/up Ratio
2	SourceIP	30	FwdIATMin	58	Average Packet Size
3	Source Port	31	Bwd IAT Total	59	Avg Fwd Segment Size
4	DestinationIP	32	Bwd IAT Mean	60	Avg Bwd Segment Size
5	DestinationPort	33	Bwd IAT Std	61	Fwd Header Length
6	Flow	34	Bwd IAT Max	62	Fwd Avg Bytes /Bulk

7	Duration	35	Bwd IAT Min	63	Fwd Avg Packets/Bulk
8	Total fwd packets	36	Fwd PSH Flags	64	Fwd Avg Bulk Rate
9	Total Backward packets	37	Bwd PSH Flags	65	Bwd Avg Bytes /Bulk
10	Total length Bwd Packets	38	Fwd URG Flags	66	Bwd Avg Packets/bulk
11	Total length of Bwd packets	39	Bwd URG Flags	67	Bwd Avg Bulk Rate
12;	Fwd Packet length max	40	Fwd header length	68	Subflow Fwd packets
13	Fwd Packet Length	41	Bwd Header Length	69	Subflow Fwd Bytes
14	Min Fwd Packet Length	42	Fwd Packets	70	Subflow Bwd Bytes
15	Mean Fwd Packet Length	43	Bwd Packet/s	71	Subflow Bwd Bytes
16	StdBwd Packet Length	44	Min Packet Length	72	Init_win _bytes_forwards
17	MaxBwd Packet Length	45	Max Packet Length	73	Init_win _bytes_forward
18	In Bwd Packet Length	46	Packet Length Mean	74	Act_data _pkt_fwd
19	Mean Bwd Packet length	47	Packet Length Std	75	Min_seq _size_forward
20	StdFlow Byte/s	48	Packet Length Variance	76	Active mean
21	Flow Packets	49	FIN Flag Count	77	Active std
22	Flow IAT Mean	50	SYN Flag Count	78	Active max

23	Flow IAT Max	51	RST Flag Count	79	Active Min
24	Flow IAT Max	52	PSH Flag Count	80	Idle Mean
25	Flow IAT Min	53	ACK Flag Count	81	Idle Std
26	Fwd IAT Total	54	URG Flag Count	82	Idle Max
27	Fwd IAT mean	55	CWE Flag Count	83	Idle Min
28	Fwd IAT Std	56	ECE Flag Count	84	Label

This file provides a labelled network traffic flow gathered using the CICFlowMeter software[34] during a certain time period. The source and destination IP addresses, timestamps, source and destination ports, protocols, and attacks were among the 83 attributes collected from the pcap log's contents. The label is the 84th feature.

The CICIDS2017 dataset comprises a variety of attacks, including PortScan, brute force, botnet, heart attack, DoS assault, web attack, and DDoS attack. After integrating all.csv files, the dataset has 2830751 records.

Table 5.7: CICIDS Attack Information

Attack Category	**Attack Types**	**Remarks**
Port Scan	Port Scan	By sending packets with changing destination ports, the attacker attempts to obtain information about the target computer, such as the operating system type and currently running service.
DOS	DoS Hulk, DDos, DoS Slow lories,Dos	The Attacker tries to perform denial o service attacks

	Slow HTTP Test, HeartBleed,Dos Golden Eye	
Brute Force	FTP Patator,SSH Patator	Patator is being used by the attacker in an effort to bruteforce the login password.
Bot	Botnet	As a result of Trojans, the attacker takes control of numerous victims' machines and arranges them into a bot network that may be abused and controlled remotely by attackers.
Web Attack	Website Brute Force, Website XSS, and Website SQL Injection	A web application that delivers malicious scripts is used by the attacker to get access to sensitive information or to insert malicious code into otherwise innocent and trustworthy websites.
Normal	Benign	Normal Traffic Flow

The CICIDS2017 dataset demonstrates some of the characteristics of the intrusion detection dataset but has a few problems. The fact that the information was divided into eight different files may be cause for worry, since processing individual files is inefficient and time intensive. As the combined data grows in bulk, overloading and processing inefficiencies occur. Even the distribution of identified assaults in the data set contributes to the data set's high-class imbalances. [34]

Table 5.7 details the CICIDS attack categories, which include port scan, denial of service, brute force, and bot. Trojans are used to compromise the security of a large number of target PCs. They take control of the devices and arrange them into a botnet that can be abused and managed remotely.

UNSW dataset

The UNSW-NB 15 dataset was created from raw network packets produced in the Australian Center for Cyber Security's (ACCS) Cyber Range Lab using the IXIA Perfect Storm platform to mix current normal operations with synthetic contemporary attack behaviour. UNSW NB15 Dataset features are given in table 5.8 and table 5.9 gives attack information in the same dataset.

Table 5.8: UNSW NB 15 Dataset Features

Feature No,	Name of the feature	Feature No.	Name of the feature
1	Srcip	26	Res_bdy_len
2	Sport	27	Sjt
3	Dstip	28	Djt
4	Dsport	29	Stime
5	Proto	30	Ltime
6	State	31	Sinpkt
7	Dur	32	Dinpkt
8	Sbytes	33	Tcprtt
9	Dbytes	34	Synack
10	Sttl	35	Ack dat
11	Dtl	36	Is_sm_ips_pos
12	Sloss	37	Ct_state_ttl
13	Doss	38	Ct_flw_http_t
14	Service	39	Is_ftp_login
15	Sload	40	Ct ftp cmd
16	Dload	41	Ct_srv_src
17	Spkts	42	Ct_sw_dst
18	Dpkts	43	Ct_dst_ltm
19	Swink	44	Ct_src_ltm
20	Dwin	45	Ct_src_dport_ltm
21	Stcpb	46	Ct_dst_dport_ltm
22	Dtcpb	47	Ct dst src ltm
23	Smeansz	48	Attack_cat
24	Dmeansz	49	Label
25	Trans_depth		

Tcpdump was used to capture 100 GB of network traffic (e.g., Pcap files). The nine categories of intrusion detected by Pcap data gathering include general, surveillance, denial-of-service, exploits, fuzzers, research, backdoors, shellcode, and worms. To produce a total of 49 characters using the Argus and Bro-IDS tools and a class name. Additionally, this utilised this dataset in our analysis. Table 6 details the numerous attacks found in the UNSW dataset.

Table 5.9: UNSW Attack Information

Attack Category	Attack Types	Remarks
Scanning	Reconnaissance, worms	This collects basic information about any public network or target host and then leverages that knowledge to access target hosts or networks using attack methods.
Seizure	DOS	The Attacker attempts denial-of-service assaults.
Penetration	Backdoor,Generic,Shell code,, Analysis,Exploits	Numerous input methods like as floppy discs or CD-ROMs, downloads, e-mail, or exploitation of known defects and security holes in applications such as Internet browsers are used to distribute these dangerous payloads..

T-Distributed Stochastic Neighboring Entities (t-SNE)

Table 5.3 visualises high-dimensional datasets in NSL KDD, CICIDS 2017, and UNSW15 using T-Distributed Stochastic Neighboring Entities (t-SNE). By translating these three datasets into matrices with pairwise similarity information, this utilised t-SNE to display high-dimensional data including these three datasets. This visualisation enabled the identification of clusters among the data points in the data set. When appropriate classification techniques are used, these clusters (if they exist) represent the true IDs. One of the data set's global characteristics

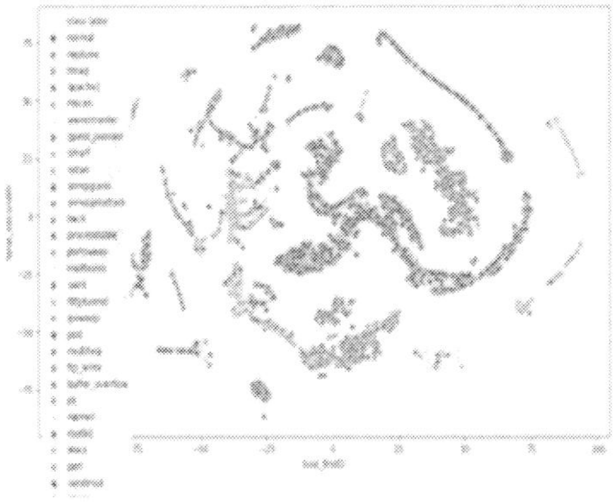

(a) t-SNE visualization of NSL KDD

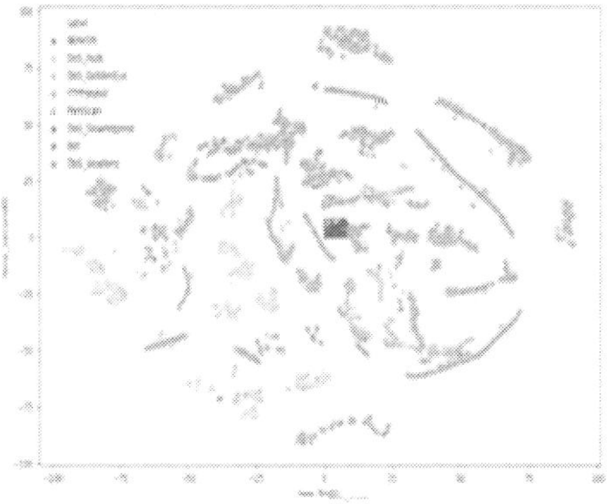

(b) t-SNE visualization of CICIDS2017

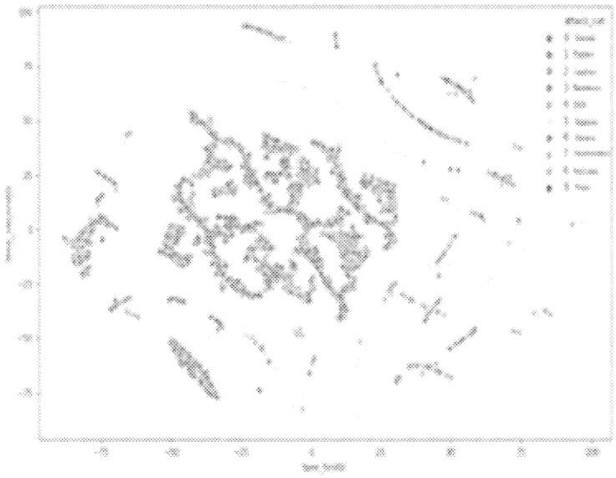

(c) t-SNE visualization of UNSW

Figure 5.3: t-SNE visualization grahs of Dataset

is the occurrence of inter- and intra-cluster variance at several sizes. This recognise that datasets are extremely skewed. The results imply that pixel-based data visualisations do not distinguish between different types of attacks. Figure 5.3.a gives t-SNE visualization of NSL KDD dataset, Figure 5.3.b gives t-SNE visualization of CICIDS 2017 dataset, Figure 5.3.c gives t-SNE visualization of UNSW NB 15 dataset. This high dimensional visualization gives details of features distributed in the dataset will cause the issue of Class imbalanced problem.

5.3.2 Imbalanced Classification

Problem of Imbalanced classifications, which is classification built with the assumption that each class had an equally large sample size. Models with low prediction accuracy, especially for minorities, are the outcome of this[118]. Typically, the minority class has a greater impact on the issue, which makes it more vulnerable to categorization mistakes for the minority class than for the majority class.There are various techniques exist to solve problem of imbalanced classification for machine learning algorithm like Random Under sampling , Random Oversampling and Synthetic Minority Oversampling Technique (SMOTE).

SMOTE: One of the most widely used oversampling approaches to overcome the imbalance problem is SMOTE (synthetic minority oversampling technique). Its goal is to achieve a more balanced distribution of classes by replicating minority class examples at random. SMOTE creates new minority instances by combining existing minorities. For the minority class, it uses linear interpolation to create virtual training records. For each example in the minority class, these synthetic training records are constructed by randomly selecting one or more of the k-nearest neighbours. The data is reconstructed after the oversampling procedure, and many classification models can be applied to the processed data.

Random undersampling: Random undersampling is the process of randomly picking and eliminating samples from the majority class from the training dataset. The majority class instances are eliminated at random until a more balanced distribution is attained in the random under-sampling method.

Random oversampling: Random oversampling is the process of randomly picking and replacing instances from the minority class in the training dataset. Random undersampling removes samples from the majority class from the training dataset at random.

Class weights calculation In our research work, class weight is calculated shown in below Algorithm 6 for each features using functions and according to class weight, train the CNN model so it solve the problem of class imbalanced.

Algorithm 5: An algorithm of solution of class imbalanced problem

1 import compute class weight from sklearn.utils.class weight

2 print(y train)

3 weights = compute class weight('balanced', np.unique(y train), y train)

4 print("***********weights**********")

5 print(weights)

6 history=cnn.fit(X train, y train, epochs=100, callbacks=[checkpointer], validation data=(X test, y test),class weight=weights)

5.3.3 NSL KDD Dataset - Preprocessing steps

Data packets include a variety of properties, including protocol type, operation, and flag, as well as a variety of features, including content features, intrinsic features, time-based features, and host-based features. The suggested system conducts data normalisation and data encoding as part of the pre-processing of the data collected during work.

1. Encoding of data: In the NSL KDD dataset, the attributes Protocol type(2), Service(3), Flag(4), and Label(42) contain a categorical value that is not numerical; data encoding is employed to convert these to numerical values.

le_x =LabelEncoder()

X[:,]=le_x.fit transform(X[:,])

here X is the dataset

Data Normalization: The attributes' values are normalised to a defined range. Sklearn was used in our analysis to do pre-processing and to get access to the Normalization function. scaler = Normalizer (). fit(X)- First, this function fits the data and then transforms it. testT= scaler.transform(X) Scale each non zero row of X to unit form Here are some data samples that are contained in NSLKDD:

Data samples of NSL KDD dataset:

Sample 1 '0', 'icmp', 'ecr i', 'SF', '9876', '1', '0', '6', '0', '0', '0', '0', '0', '0', '0', '0', '0', '0', '0', '0', '0', '0', '0', '0', '511', '511', '0.00', '0.00', '0.00', '0.00', '1.00', '0.00', '0.00', '255', '255', '1.00', '0.00', '1.00', '0.00', '0.00', '0.00', '0.00', '0.00', 'smurf.'

Sample 2 '0', 'udp', 'http', 'SF', '7680', '1234', '0', '4', '0', '2', '0', '1', '1', '0', '0', '0', '0', '0', '0', '0', '0', '0', '5', '5', '0.00', '0.00', '0.20', '0.20',

'1.00', '0.00', '0.00', '220', '220', '1.00', '0.00', '0.00', '0.00', '0.00', '0.00', '0.06', '0.06', 'back.'

Sample 3 '0', 'tcp', 'http', 'SF', '567', '769', '0', '0', '0', '0', '0', '1', '0', '0', '0', '0', '0', '0', '0', '0', '0', '0', '9', '14', '0.00', '0.00', '0.00', '0.00', '1.00', '0.00', '0.14', '255', '255', '1.00', '0.00', '0.00', '0.00', '0.00', '0.00', '0.00', '0.00', 'normal.'

5.3.4 CICIDS2017 Dataset - Preprocessing steps

The CICIDS2017 dataset was subjected to the following pre-processing in order to make it suitable for the research.

1. Using the col. replace (", ") function, remove whitespaces from column names. The regular expressions will be used to replace unusual characters such as /, " with dunders. System replaced the function with a regular expressions library and sub.
2. Given that just 334 rows in the total dataset contain NULL values, or around 0.01 percent, system may securely delete all NULL rows without contaminating the data using the dropna function.
3. System tested the dataset for endless values and replaced them with NaN values.
4. Subsequently, the same processes of encoding and normalisation as for the NSL-KDD dataset were performed in the research.

Data samples of CICIDS2017 dataset:

Sample 1

54865, 3, 2, 0, 12, 0, 6, 6, 6, 0, 0, 0, 0, 0, 4000000, 666666.6667, 3, 0, 3, 3, 3, 3, 0, 3, 3, 0, 0, 0, 0, 0, 0, 0, 0, 0, 40, 0, 666666.6667, 0, 6, 6, 6, 0, 0 0, 0, 0, 0, 1, 0, 0, 0, 0, 9, 6, 0, 40, 0, 0, 0, 0, 0, 0, 2, 12, 0, 0, 33, -1, 1, 20, 0, 0, 0, 0, 0, 0, 0, 0, BENIGN,

Sample 2

80, 1293792, 3, 7, 26, 11607, 20, 0, 8.666666667, 10.26320288, 5840, 0, 1658.142857, 2137.29708, 8991.398927, 7.72921768, 143754.6667, 430865.8067, 1292730, 2, 747, 373.5, 523.9661249, 744, 3, 1293746, 215624.3333, 527671.9348, 1292730, 2, 0, 0, 0, 0, 72, 152, 2.318765304, 5.410452376, 0, 5840, 1057.545455, 1853.437529, 3435230.673, 0, 0, 0, 1, 0, 0, 0, 0, 2, 1163.3, 8.666666667, 1658.142857, 72, 0, 0, 0, 0, 0, 3, 26, 7, 11607, 8192, 229, 2, 20, 0, 0, 0, 0, 0, 0, 0, 0, DDoS,

Sample 3

21 20 1 1 0 0 0 0 0 0 0 0 0 0 0 0 100000 20 0 20 20 0 0 0 0 0 0 0 0 0 0 0 0 0 0 0 32 32 50000 50000 0 0 0 0 0 0 0 0 0 0 1 1 0 0 1 0 0 0 32 0 0 0 0 0 0 1 0 1 0 229 227 0 32 0 0 0 0 0 0 0 0 FTP-Patator

5.3.5 UNSW NB 15 Dataset - Preprocessing steps

The UNSW Dataset was pre-processed by the following ways:

The "ID" property was eliminated since it serves as a serial number for the entries in our method's initial step.

Label encoding was applied on a subset of the dataset's features in order to create identical features.

Additionally, normalisation was used to scale a value to a particular range of characteristics. 4.Because some of the features in the UNSW dataset have a fixed value, data encoding is utilised to convert them to numerical values; as with the NSL KDD dataset, system do normalisation and label encoding in the same way.

Data samples of UNSW NB 15 dataset:

Sample 1

0.000011 , udp , INT , 2 , 0 , 496 , 0 , 90909.0902 , 254 , 0 , 180363632 0 0 0 0.011 0 0 0 0 0 0 0 0 0 0 248 , 0 , 0 , 0 , 2 , 2 , 1 , 1 , 1 , 2 , 0 , 0 , 0 , 1 , 2 , 0 , Normal

Sample 2

0.000009 sctp INT 2 0 104 0 111111.1072 254 0 46222220 0 0 0 0.009 0 0 0 0 0 0 0 0 0 0 52 0 0 0 1 2 2 1 1 2 0 0 0 1 1 0 Exploits

Sample 3

0.209133, tcp, http, FIN, 10, 6, 508, 268, 71.724692, 254, 252, 17519.95117, 8568.709961, 2,

1, 21.766333, 32.622801, 1139.187144, 51.108875, 255, 3869127034, 1987960674, 255, 0.066589,

0.046011, 0.020578, 51, 45, 1, 0, 12, 1, 2, 2, 1, 12, 0, 0, 1, 2, 12, 0, Fuzzers

5.3.6 Feature Extraction

To get accurate results, it is important to pull out characteristics. Many dimensionality reduction methods are used to get rid of properties in network traffic data that aren't useful or are repeated. The CNN is used to automatically extract from the dimensionality reduction data the properties listed in Table 5.10, which leads to better information about how to find intrusions. Maximum pooling picks the most important element in the filter's feature map area. So, the feature map would draw attention to the most important features. In multi-class classification problems, the loss function is shown by the sparse categorical cross-entropy. The softmax layer gives each label a probability distribution.

Table 5.10,5.11,5.12 shows important features Extracted using CNN from NSL KDD dataset, CICIDS Dataset, UNSW Dataset respectively.

Table 5.10: Important Features of NSL KDD Dataset

Sr. No.	Feature No	Feature Name
1	F9	urgent
2	F8	wrong_fragent
3	F7	land
4	F6	dst-bytes
5	F5	src_bytes
6	F40	dst_host_rerror_rate
7	F4	flag
8	F39	Dst-host-srv-serror-rate
9	F38	dst-host-serror-rate
10	F37	dst-host-srv-diff-host-rate
11	F36	dst-host-same-src-port
12	F35	dst-host-diff-srv-rate

Table 5.11: Important Features of CICIDS2017 Dataset

Sr. No.	Feature No	Feature Name
1	F9	fwd packet length std
2	F8	fwd packet length mean
3	F7	fwd packet length min
4	F6	fwd packet length max
5	F5	Total length of bwd packet
6	F4	Total length of fwd packet
7	F3	Total bwd packet
8	F2	Total fwd packet

Sr. No.	Feature No	Feature Name
9	F15	Flow packet/s
10	F14	Flow byte/s
11	F13	Bwd packet length std
12	F12	Bwd packet length mean

Table 5.12: Important Features of UNSW 15

Sr. No.	Feature No	Feature Name
1	F9	Rate
2	F8	Sttl
3	F7	Dltl
4	F6	dpkts
5	F5	spkts
6	F40	ct-src-ltm
7	F4	State
8	F39	ct-flw-http-mthd
9	F38	ct-ftp-cmd
10	F37	is-ftp-login
11	F36	ct-dst-src-ltm
12	F35	ct-dst-sport-ltm

5.4 Detection Engine

5.5 Deep learning algorithm

Deep learning algorithms are classified into three categories: supervised, semi-supervised, and unsupervised [1]. Deep learning techniques outperform classical machine learning algorithms, including distributed soft computing, in detecting intrusions. Convolutional Neural Networks (CNNs) are a subcategory of deep neural networks. Machine learning algorithms need human feature extraction in order to provide novel insights. Detailed system architecture is given in Figure

5.4, which consist of training and testing module , in training phase model is trained with 80% of dataset and 20% is used for testing of dataset. All the steps are explained in the last section.

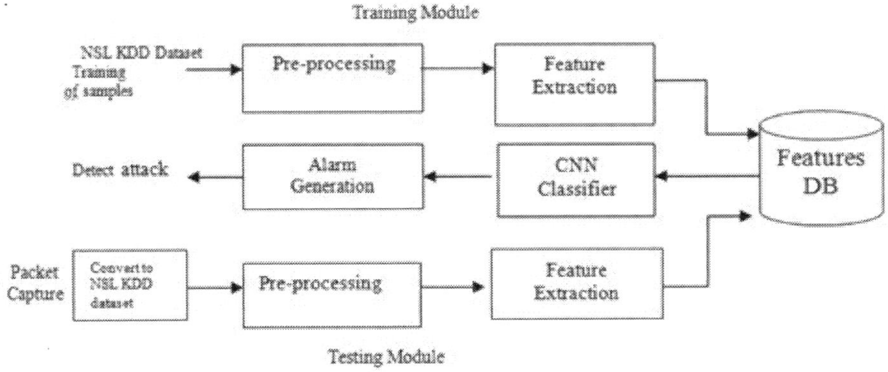

Figure 5.4: Anomaly Based IDS

5.5.1 Convolutional Neural Network Architecture

The Convolutional neural network (CNN) is a well-known structure created for processing complex data in deep learning neural networks. The CNN, which is primarily utilised in this IDS to overcomes the typical constraints of conventional machine learning methodologies of feature extraction and improved the accuracy in detection of attack.

In general, a CNN has three layers: the convolutional layer, the pooling layer, and the fully connected layer.

By using 2D Convolutional layers, CNN gets rid of the need to physically extract features. CNN is often used to directly pull feature vectors out of a dataset. CNN gets the characteristics of the dataset. As the number of layers stacked up goes up, the accuracy goes up in a straight line. Microsoft Research came up with ResNet, which uses skip connections to make deeper models, to solve this problem (also known as shortcut connections or residuals). Residual Networks were used in our intrusion detection method to solve the problem of gradients disappearing or exploding.

1. Convolution Layer The convolutional layer is the fundamental component of the CNN. It is responsible for the majority of the network's computational burden. This layer conducts a dot product on two matrices, one of which represents the set of learnable parameters, referred to as a kernel, and the other of which represents the limited section of the receptive field. Kernels are geographically smaller than images yet have a greater depth. This implies that if a picture is formed of three (RGB) channels, the kernel height and width will be minimal in terms of spatial dimensions, but the depth will span all three channels.

2. Pooling Layer The pooling layer substitutes for the network's output at certain points by computing a summary statistic for the neighbouring outputs. This aids in lowering the representation's spatial size, which in turn reduces the amount of computation and weights necessary. Each slice of the representation is treated independently during the pooling phase. There are numerous pooling functions available, including the rectangle neighborhood's average, the rectangular neighborhood's L2 norm, and a weighted average depending on the distance from the centre pixel. However, the most frequent approach is max pooling, which reports the neighborhood's maximum output.

3. Fully Connected Layer As is the case with ordinary FCNN, neurons in this layer have complete connection to all neurons in the previous and following layers. This is why, as is customary, it may be estimated using matrix multiplication and a bias effect. The FC layer contributes to the representation mapping between the input and output.

4. Non-Linearity Layers Due to the fact that convolution is a linear operation and pictures are anything but linear, non-linearity layers are often added right after the convolutional layer to bring non-linearity into the activation map.

Table 5.13: CNN Model details

CNN Models	**Year**	**Novel**
LeeNet5	1998	A method of building networks by connecting all of the convolutions and pooling layers at the top.
AlexNet	2012	Rectified Linear Units were the major activation functions (ReLUs).
VGG-16	2014	The input came from a more extensive network (roughly twice as deep as AlexNet).
Inception-v1	2014	As opposed to stocking these modules, they are shown as stack modules or blocks inside Convolutionary layers.
ResNet-50	2015	They made skip connections more popular. Up to 152 layers can be added to a CNN so that the model can be used to generalise. When batch normalisation came out. When the network's depth grows, it can avoid the Gradient explosion.

This study implements IDS using a Convolutional Neural Network model ResNet 50(CNN), which provides an improvement over standard machine learning approaches, which are insufficient to lower the false alarm rate. The suggested intrusion detection system (IDS) concept detects network intrusions by classifying every network packet traffic as legitimate or malicious. Details of all the CNN model is given in the Table 5.13. In comparison to well-known CNNs such as AlexNet [16] and LeNet-5 [25]. ResNets were used to create the Neural Network. Deeper networks are routinely built as a result of the fact that the depth of a CNN has a major effect on its ability to predict events. One of the problems is the Gradient explosion that occurs as the network depth increases, resulting in a decrease in the network's output[122]. For convolutions and layer pooling, LeeNet5 is "template" standard, and the network is completed with one or more layers that are completely linked. Rectified Linear Units (RLUs) are AlexNet's principal activation functions (ReLUs). VGG-16 made a significant contribution to the development of deeper networking (roughly twice as deep as AlexNet). Inception-v1 instead of stocking modules or blocks, stacks them inside Convolutionary layers. It is possible to create deeper CNNs (up to 152 layers) without impairing the model's ability to generalise, thanks to the popularisation of ResNet-50. When the depth of the network increases, batch normalisation was one of the first methods to prevent the Gradient explosion.

To calculate the feature maps of a convolutional layer built by a filter f in the i-th input element of the ResNet50 model, we need to know the specific dimensions and parameters of the model, as well as the size and shape of the input data. The ResNet50 model takes as input tensor of size (batch size, height, width, channels), where batch size is the number of examples in each batch, and height, width, and channels represent the dimensions of the packet data. Let's consider the example of the first convolutional layer in the ResNet50 model, which has a filter size of 7x7, a stride of 2, and 64 output channels. The calculation of the feature map of this layer for a specific input element i can be expressed as follows:

$$H_{i,f,:,:} = \sigma\left(\sum_{j=1}^{7}\sum_{k=1}^{7}(x_{i+(j-1)*2,k+(k-1)*2,:} \cdot kf_{j,k,:,:}) + bf\right) \quad (5.1)$$

where: • $H_{i,f,:,:}$ is the feature map of the i-th input element and the f-th filter • σ is the activation function • $x_{i+(j-1)*2,k+(k-1)*2,:}$ represents a sub-matrix of the input data, of size (7, 7, 3), centered at the i-th input element and shifted by the j-th and k-th offsets, with a stride of 2 in both dimensions • $kf_{j,k,:,:}$ is the trainable convolution kernel of the f-th filter for the (j,k)-th position in the kernel, with size (7, 7, 3, 64) • bf is the trainable bias term of the f-th filter, with size (64)

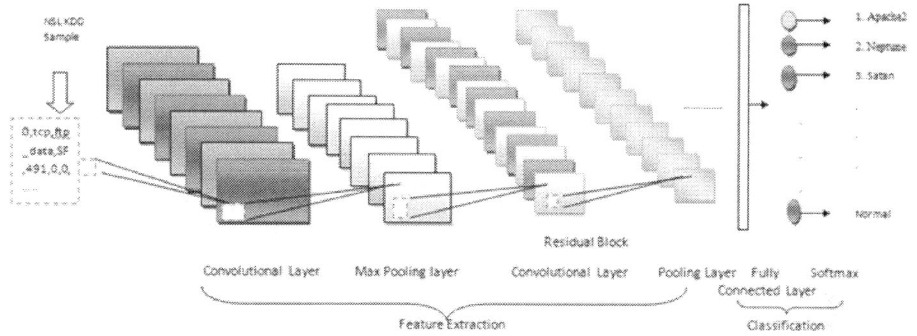

Figure 5.5: ResNet 50 CNN proposed module

Figure 5.5 shows the recommended ResNet 50 CNN model. A convolution layer, a max-pooling layer, a residual block, feature extraction pooling layers, a fully connected layer, and a softmax function or classification layer make up this algorithm. The algorithm is in-depth.

ResNet block

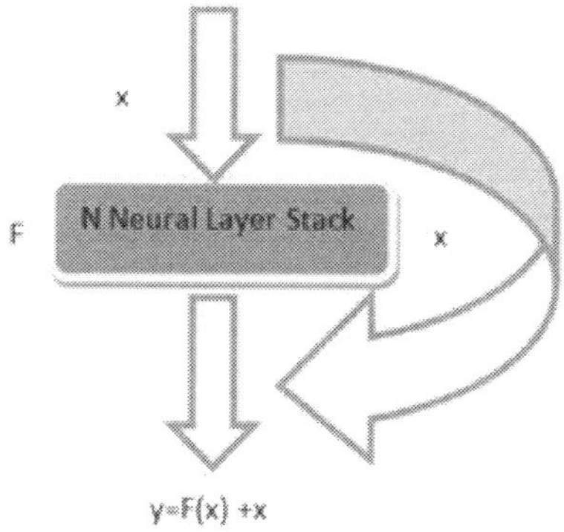

Figure 5.6: ResNet Block

It is used to solve problems through residual learning. Residual blocks are those that do not link to one another. They discover residual functions for layer inputs.

The ResNet block is seen in Figure 5.6. The batch normalisation is then applied in layers to the SKIP connection, beginning with the Convolution layer. The building of residual blocks revolves on a link known as a skip connection.

Algorithm for ResNet 50 This below Algorithm 7 explained ResNet 50 evaluated on three datasets UNSW NB 2015 dataset, NSL KDD dataset, CICIDS 2017 dataset.

The residual is the difference between the local input and the output, as illustrated in equation 5.1.

$$f(x) = g(x) - x \tag{5.2}$$

In (5.2) g(x) denotes the stacked nonlinear layers, whereas x denotes the identity function (input=output).

Training data to Algorithm 7 are UNSW NB 2015 dataset, NSL KDD dataset, CICIDS 2017 dataset. Steps are the following

Step 1: Constructed a sequential model.

Algorithm 6: ResNet50 Convolutional Neural Network

Require: Input Image I
Require: Number of classes C
Require: Learning rate α
Require: Batch size B
Require: Number of epochs E

$conv1 \leftarrow Conv2D(64, (7,7), strides = (2,2), padding =' same')(I)$
$bn1 \leftarrow BatchNormalization()(conv1)$
$relu1 \leftarrow Activation('relu')(bn1)$
$maxpool1 \leftarrow MaxPooling2D((3,3), strides = (2,2), padding =' same')(relu1)$
$res2a \leftarrow identity_block(maxpool1, 64)$
$res2b \leftarrow projection_block(res2a, 64)$
$res2c \leftarrow identity_block(res2b, 64)$
$res3a \leftarrow identity_block(res2c, 128)$
$res3b \leftarrow projection_block(res3a, 128)$
$res3c \leftarrow identity_block(res3b, 128)$
$res3d \leftarrow identity_block(res3c, 128)$
$res4a \leftarrow identity_block(res3d, 256)$
$res4b \leftarrow projection_block(res4a, 256)$
$res4c \leftarrow identity_block(res4b, 256)$
$res4d \leftarrow identity_block(res4c, 256)$
$res4e \leftarrow identity_block(res4d, 256)$
$res4f \leftarrow identity_block(res4e, 256)$
$res5a \leftarrow identity_block(res4f, 512)$
$res5b \leftarrow projection_block(res5a, 512)$
$res5c \leftarrow identity_block(res5b, 512)$
$avgpool \leftarrow AveragePooling2D((7,7))(res5c)$
$flatten \leftarrow Flatten()(avgpool)$
$fc \leftarrow Dense(C, activation =' softmax')(flatten)$
$model \leftarrow Model(inputs = I, outputs = fc)$
$model.compile(optimizer = Adam(lr = \alpha), loss =' categorical_crossentropy', metrics = ['accuracy'])$

```
for i = 1 to E do
    loss ← 0
    acc ← 0
    for j = 1 to N/B do
        X ← Random batch of size B
        Y ← Labels for X
        metrics ← model.train_on_batch(X, Y)
        loss ← loss + metrics[0]
        acc ← acc + metrics[1]
    end for
    loss ← loss / (N/B)
    acc ← acc / (N/B)
    Print epoch i, loss loss, accuracy acc
end for
```

Step 2: Conv1D's convolutional neural layers were generated using a single module.

Step 3: Relu-based individual layer activation has been added. The activation function Relu was used to overcome the vanishing gradient problem and allow models to learn.

Step 4: It was batch normalised. By ensuring that the input to each layer has the same distribution, batch normalisation lowers the difficulty of network training.

Step 5: The addition of the MaxPooling layer produced a feature map by extracting spatial characteristics from the input data. Then, using maximum pooling, the greatest value for each patch of the function map is determined.

Step 6: Filter size 64 and kernel size 4 were used.

Step 7: The flattening layer converts the information from the preceding layers into a one-dimensional vector.

Step 8: The output size is continuously reduced by fully connected layers, and the ultimate output is determined by an activation function.

Step 9: Before feeding the output of the convolution + pooling layers into the fully connected layers, flattened it.

Step 10: Each channel in the feature map is reduced to a single value via global pooling.

Step 11: Dropout is a technique for avoiding overfitting.

Step 12: Print epochs and accuracy and loss.

The difference between input and output is decreased to zero via residual learning. To understand more about the residual, connect the original input to one layer of the Residual learning is enabled by a shortcut between two blocks, and it stops the network from being enlarged with new characteristics and calculations; it also automatically trains its parameters and guarantees that the network continues to perform properly as it learns more.

Mathematical Model of ResNet 50 CNN Model

Let x be the training dataset sample, and let f be a function that represents the ResNet-50 architecture. The output of ResNet-50 can be calculated as follows:

$$y = f(x) \tag{5.3}$$

where y is the output vector, and $f(x)$ represents the forward pass of the ResNet-50 architecture. The ResNet-50 architecture consists of multiple layers, including convolutional layers, batch normalization layers, and fully connected layers. Let L be the number of layers in the ResNet-50 architecture. Then, the output of the i-th layer can be represented as follows:

$$x_i = g_i(x_{i-1}) \tag{5.4}$$

where g_i represents the i-th layer of the ResNet-50 architecture, and x_{i-1} represents the output of the $(i-1)$-th layer. The ResNet-50 architecture also includes shortcut connections, which are used to skip over one or more layers. Let $h_i(x)$ represent the output of the shortcut connection at layer i. Then, the output of the i-th layer with shortcut connections can be represented as follows:

$$x_i = g_i(x_{i-1}) + h_i(x_{i-2}) \tag{5.5}$$

where x_{i-2} represents the output of the $(i-2)$-th layer. Finally, the output of the ResNet-50 architecture can be obtained by passing the output of the last layer through a softmax function:

$$y = softmax(x_L) \tag{5.6}$$

where x_L represents the output of the last layer, and *softmax*() represents the softmax function.

5.5.2 Result and Discussion

Using three datasets, the proposed model which is based on CNN ResNet 50 model is trained and tested using the NSL-KDD dataset, the CICIDS2017 dataset and the UNSW[125] . Activation functions its Result with 10 epochs on NSL KDD is shown in Table 5.14. Here it represents softmax activation function gives for result as compared with other activation function. Figure depicts in AIDS module result with 3 datasets. With LeeNet 5 and ResNet50's LeeNet 5, the model's overall precision, accuracy, recall and F1 score are all displayed in Table 5.15. Result analysis comparison is given in Table 5.16. Figure 5.9 depicts the AIDS module result with CNN LeeNet5 and ResNet 50 on NSL KDD Dataset.

Table 5.14: Activation functions its Result with 10 epochs on NSL KDD

Sr. No.	Activation functions	Result (10 Epochs)
1	Elu	84.36%
2	Softmax	89.59 %
3	Relu	84.36%
4	Sigmoid	87.65 %

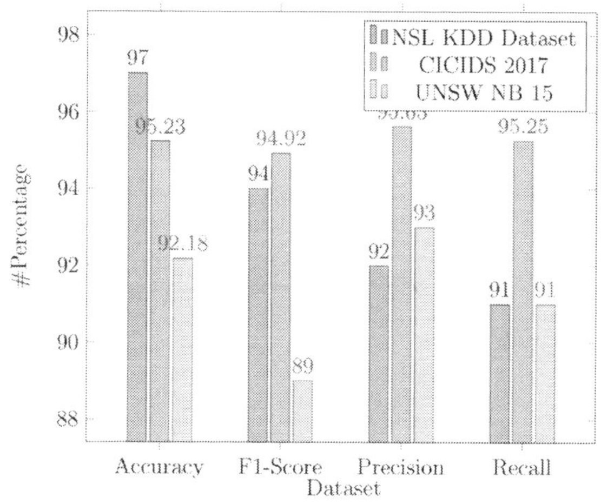

Figure 5.7: AIDS Module Result with 3 datasets

Table 5.15: Comparative Analysis of CNN ResNet 50 and CNN LeeNet 5

Parameters	CNN ResNet 50	CNN LeeNet 5
Precision	97.25	93
F1 Score	95	94
Accuracy	97.25	92.18
Recall	92	91

Table 5.16: Result Analysis

Sr. No.	Parameters	UNSW-NB 15 dataset	NSL dataset	KDD	CICIDS17 Dataset
1	Precision	93	92		95.63
2	F1 Score	89	94		94.92
3	Accuracy	92.18	97.25		95.23
4	Recall	91	91		95.25

Receiver operating characteristic curves (ROC) reveal the overall performance, as well as what level of classification is appropriate for any given detection model. This graph shows how the TPR and FPR are correlated at various thresholds. Figures 5.8(c), 5.8(a), and 5.8(b) show the ROC curves for UNSW NB-15,NSL-KDD, CICIDS 17 respectively.

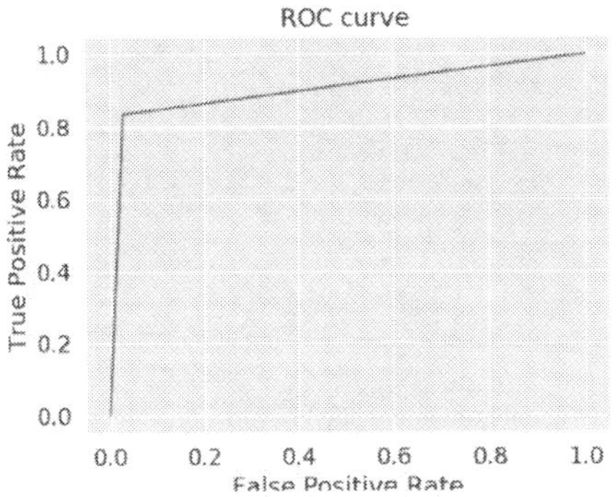

(a) ROC Curve of NSL KDD

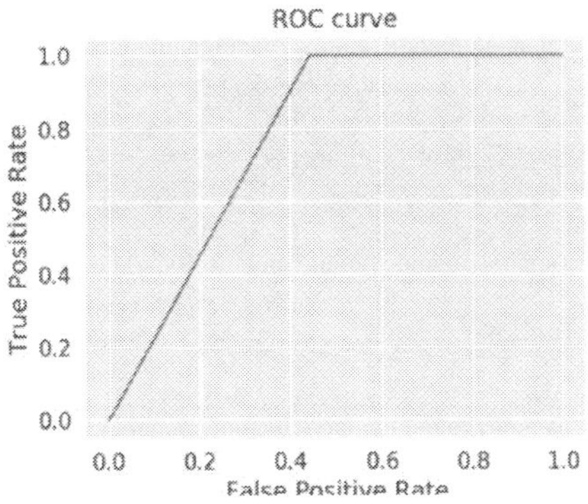

(b) ROC Curve of CICIDS2017

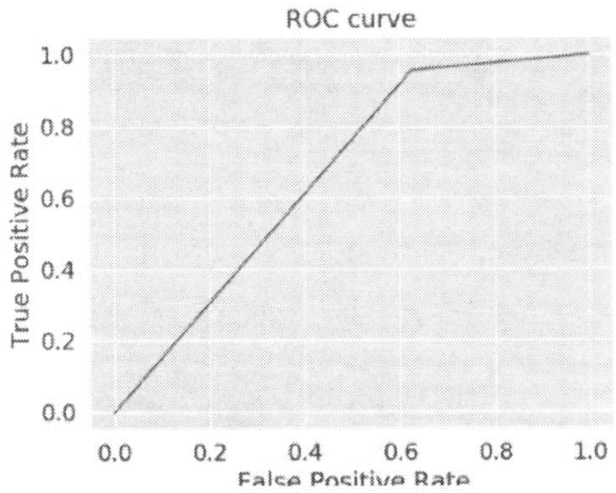

(c) ROC Curve of UNSW

Figure 5.8: ROC graphs of Dataset

5.6 Conclusion

The study found that anomaly-based intrusion detection is the most effective method for shielding a network from novel threats. Despite this, there are still concerns about its dependability due to its features. An technique to deep learning using Convolutional Neural networks called ResNet 50 is described in this chapter. We carefully

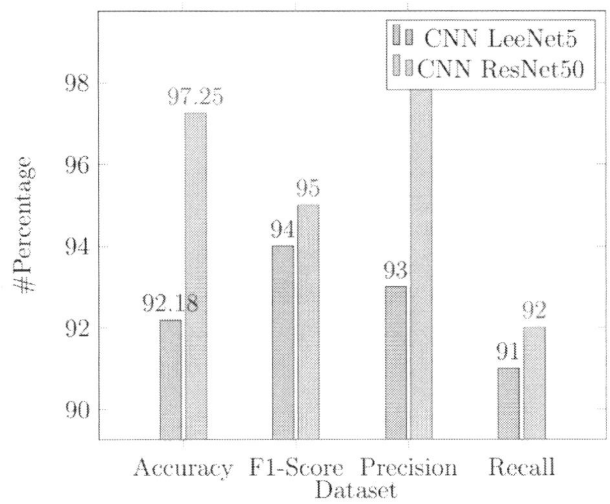

Figure 5.9: AIDS Module Result with CNN LeeNet and ResNet 50

examined the datasets commonly used to evaluate intrusion detection, NSL-KDD, CICIDS2017, and UNSWNB 15. Support vector machine (SVM), random forest (RF), k-nearest neighbour (kNN), Naive Bayes (NB), linear regression (LR), AdaBoost (AB), and decision tree (DT) were all used to compare the model to seven well-known machine learning classifiers and results are shown in Chapter 6.

6

Result And Discussion

6.1 Implementation and Performance Evaluation

6.1.1 Implementation

The Intrusion Detection System was created using Google's Tensorflow, which allows the network architecture to be seen. The trials were carried out under the following conditions: Specifications of the system: 2.20 GHz Intel ® Core TM i5-5200U CPU RAM: 8GB Operating System: Ubuntu Python Libraries: Scikit-learn, Numpy, Tensorflow, Pandas.

1. Using the LibPack library, collect realtime packets from the network.
2. Use a signature-based Rule set which can make predictions by analysing network traffic in real-time with unique signatures.
3. If the Signature-based detection engine fails to identify an attack,then control goes to the Anomaly-based detection engine, which uses the CNN ResNet50 classifier to detect anomalies.
4. If attack detected then generate alarm and shows three most probable attacks with percentages.

Tensorflow

TensorFlow is a full machine learning platform that is open source. It has a comprehensive, flexible ecosystem of tools, libraries, and community resources that enable academics to push the boundaries of machine learning while enabling developers to swiftly build and deploy ML-powered apps.

TensorFlow is a collection of processes with simple, high-level APIs that enable machine learning models to be developed in a number of languages by both beginners and experts. Models may be run on a range of platforms, including servers, the cloud, mobile and edge devices, browsers, and a number of other JavaScript platforms. This makes the transition from model creation and training to deployment more simpler for developers.

Scikit-learn

Scikit-learn offers a consistent Python interface for a range of supervised and unsupervised learning algorithms.

It's included in a number of Linux distributions and comes with a permissive simplified BSD licence that encourages academic and commercial usage.

SciPy (Scientific Python), which must be installed before using scikit-learn, is the foundation of the package. This stack is made up of the following items:

NumPy is a Python package that offers an n-dimensional array base. SciPy is a widely used scientific computing environment. Matplotlib is a 2D/3D charting toolkit with a lot of features. IPython is a more sophisticated interactive terminal based on Python. Mathematical symbols (Sympy) Pandas is a data organisation and analysis programme.

NumPy

NumPy (numerical Python) is a package that includes multidimensional array objects as well as a collection of techniques for manipulating them. NumPy can perform logical and mathematical operations on arrays. The essentials of NumPy, including its design and environment, are covered in this course. It also covers array functions, indexing algorithms, and other topics.

6.2 Evaluation Parameters

IDS must have a high detection rate in order to be effective. IDS performance cannot be evaluated only on the basis of accuracy rate. There are a number of measures that may be used to measure IDS performance, and they include:

- True Positive (TP): The number of intrusions that have been accurately identified.
- True Negative (TN): Number of successfully recognised non-intrusions
- False Positive (FP): The number of false positives for non-intrusions.
- False Negative (FN): The number of intrusions detected wrongly.

This is how it look like in graphic way:

Table 6.1: Confusion Matrix

	Prediction: No	Prediction Yes
True Value: No	TN	FP
True Value : Yes	FN	TP

A confusion matrix is a table shown in 6.1 that shows how well a classification model (or "classifier") performs on a set of test data for which the real values are known.

Accuracy is a metric that indicates the proportion of accurate detection of attacks. It is defined as "the proportion of right detection made to the total number of detection made."

$$Accuracy = \frac{TP + TN}{TP + TN + FP + FN} \tag{6.1}$$

Precision is defined as the ratio of properly categorised Positive samples of intrusion detection to total Positive samples (either correctly or incorrectly detect attacks). Precision is a metric that indicates how well a model classifies a sample as positive.

$$Precision = \frac{TP}{TP + FP} \tag{6.2}$$

The recall is determined as the ratio of properly identified Positive samples to the total number of Positive samples. The recall parameter indicates how well the model can identify Positive samples. The greater the recall, the greater the number of positive samples found.

$$Recall = \frac{TP}{TP + FN} \tag{6.3}$$

The harmonic mean of accuracy and recall, also known as the classic F-measure or balanced F-score, is a metric that combines precision and recall.

$$F1 = \frac{2 * Precision * Recall}{Precision + Recall} = \frac{2 * TP}{2 * TP + FP + FN} \tag{6.4}$$

6.2.1 Anomaly based IDS

Classical Machine learning Algorithms like Support Vector Machine, Ada Boost, K Nearest Neighbors, Decision Tree, Linear Regression,

Random Forest, Naive Bayes classifier are used to compare with the Anomaly based Model employing ResNet 50 and is shown in Table 6.2, 6.3 and 6.4 for NSL KDD dataset, CICIDS 2017 and UNSW NB 2015 Dataset respectively. Support Vector Machine (SVM) [18] [51] [54] [55] [70] [74] [79] is used to increase sample dimensionality in order to separate them. The goal is to discover a hyperplane and fill it with samples from the same class. AdaBoost[49] was one of the earliest boosting algorithms to be used in problem solving. Adaboost enables the combination of many "weak classifiers" into a single "strong classifier." Here are some (interesting) statistics on Adaboost. The Supervised Learning methodology is used in K-Nearest Neighbor[42], a fundamental Machine Learning method. The K-NN approach assumes that the new case/data and old cases are comparable and puts the new case in the most similar category to the existing categories. A decision tree [7] [56] [70] [74] [78] [80] [101] [103] [113] [122][123] [124] is a tree tree structure with each internal node representing an attribute test, each branch representing the test's conclusion, and each leaf node (terminal node) holding a class label. Random Forest (RF) [42] [48] [52] [95] uses an unpruned classification ensemble technique, transferring training data to bootstrap samples through random feature selection. Naive Bayes (NB) [43] [52] [54] [74] [82] [99] [110] is a probabilistic technique that represents a collection of random variables and their conditional interactions using a directed acyclic graph.

Features Extraction Results

The CNN is used to automatically extract from the dimensionality reduction data the properties listed in Table 5.10, which leads to better information about how to find intrusions. Maximum pooling picks the most important element in the filter's feature map area. So, the feature map would draw attention to the most important features. In multi-class classification problems, the loss function is shown by the sparse categorical cross-entropy. The softmax layer gives each label a probability distribution. A box and whisker plot is a structured, prepared form for collecting and analyzing data. Important features selected by CNN model for 3 datasets like NSL - KDD dataset, UNSW NB 15 dataset, CICIDS 2017 Dataset are shown with Box and Whisker plots with descriptive statistics are given below.

Table 6.2: Comparative Analysis NSL KDD Dataset

Algorithm	Accuracy	Precision	Recall	F1-score
Support Vector Machine	0.702	0.689	0.702	0.656
Ada Boost	0.621	0.651	0.621	0.594
K-nearest Neighbors	0.731	0.720	0.731	0.684
Decision Tree	0.763	0.767	0.763	0.728
Linear Regression	0.612	0.509	0.612	0.530
Random Forest	0.753	0.814	0.753	0.715
Naive Bayes	0.295	0.297	0.295	0.184
ResNet 50 Model	0.9765	0.92	0.91	0.94

Table 6.3: Comparative Analysis CICIDS 2017 Dataset

Algorithm	Accuracy	Precision	Recall	F1-score
K-nearest Neighbors	0.909	0.949	0.909	0.922
Support Vector Machine	0.799	0.757	0.799	0.723
Ada Boost	0.641	0.691	0.641	0.653
Linear Regression	0.870	0.889	0.870	0.868
Decision Tree	0.940	0.965	0.940	0.949
Random Forest	0.944	0.970	0.944	0.953
Naive Bayes	0.250	0.767	0.250	0.188
ResNet 50 Model	0.9523	0.9563	0.9523	0.9492

Table 6.4: Comparative Analysis UNSW 15 Dataset

Algorithm	Accuracy	Precision	Recall	F1-score
Support Vector Machine	0.581	0.586	0.581	0.496
Decision Tree	0.733	0.721	0.733	0.705
Random Forest	0.755	0.755	0.755	0.724
Linear Regression	0.538	0.414	0.538	0.397
Naive Bayes	0.437	0.579	0.437	0.396
Ada Boost	0.608	0.502	0.608	0.526
K-nearest Neighbors	0.622	0.578	0.622	0.576
ResNet 50 Model	0.9218	0.93	0.91	0.89

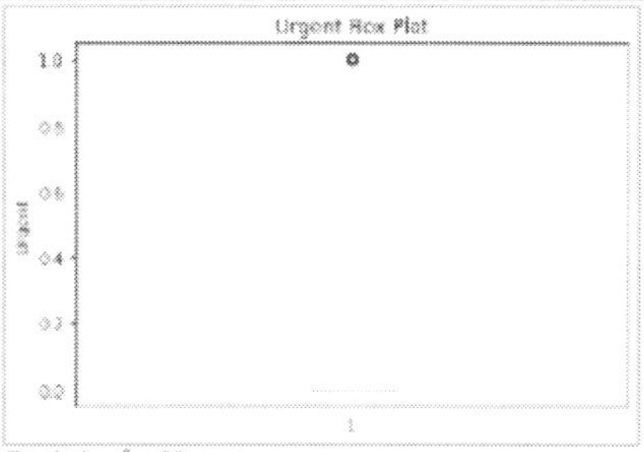

Statistics for Urgent
Standard deviation: 0.16620720280615295
Mean: 0.028433286018452804
Max: 1
Mode: 0
Median: 0.0

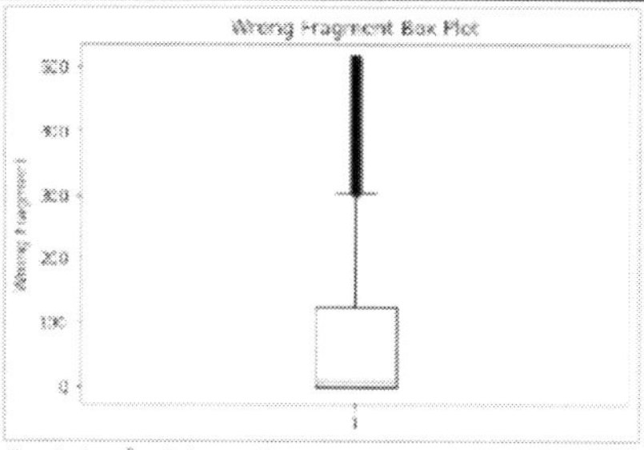

Statistics for Wrong Fragment
Standard deviation: 128.53639696429414
Mean: 79.02834457061746
Max: 511
Mode: 1
Median: 8.0

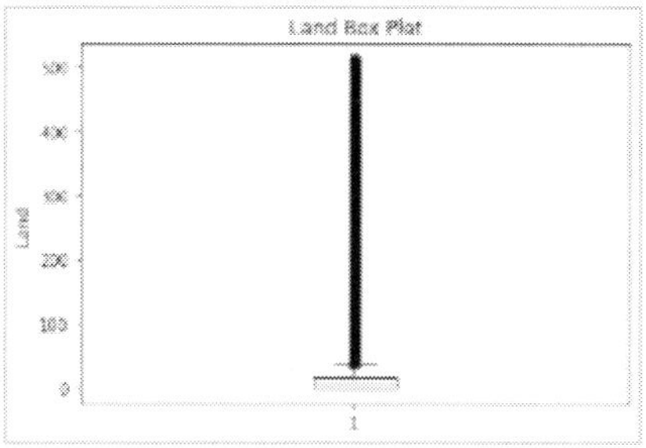

Statistics for Land
Standard deviation: 89.06055637783227
Mean: 31.124378992193044
Max: 511
Mode: 1
Median: 6.0

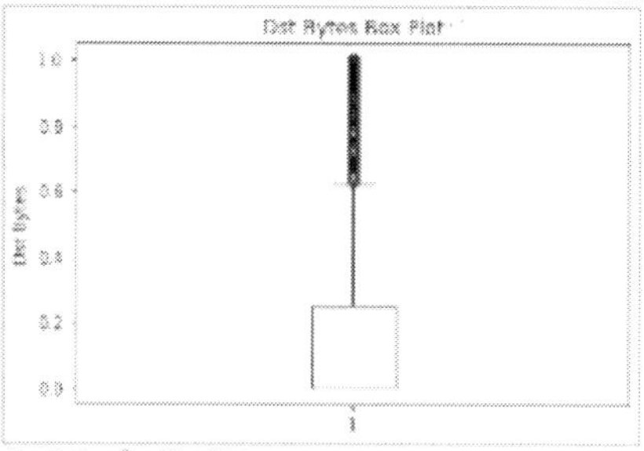

Statistics for Dst Bytes
Standard deviation: 0.41610841588012554
Mean: 0.2384630056778567
Max: 1.0
Mode: 0.0
Median: 0.0

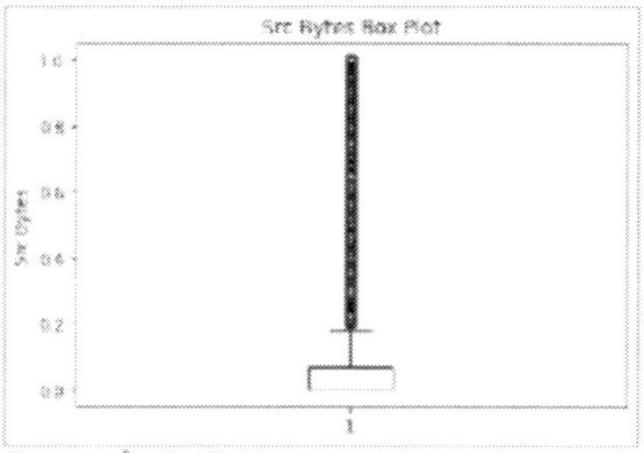

Statistics for Src Bytes
Standard deviation: 0.41620571211947494
Mean: 0.235178761533300207
Max: 1.0
Mode: 0.0

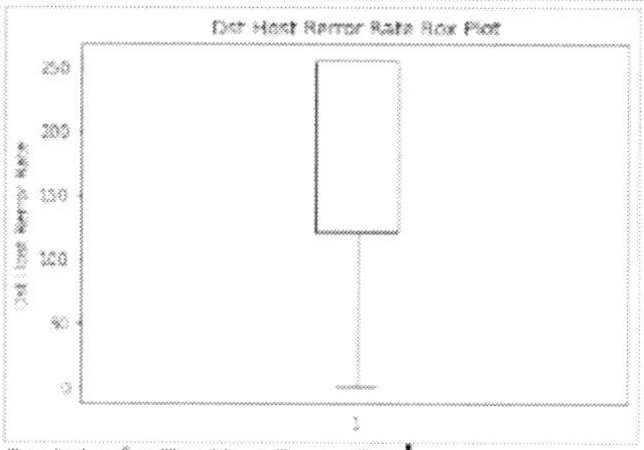

Statistics for Dst Host Rerror Rate
Standard deviation: 94.03357739398002
Mean: 193.8694109297374
Max: 255
Mode: 255

Figure 6.1: Box and Whisker Plot of NSl KDD important Features Part1

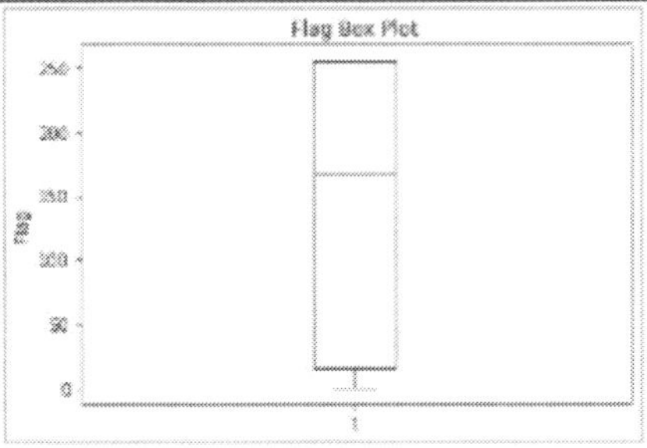

Statistics for Flag
Standard deviation: 111.78149290245192
Mean: 140.75053229240595
Max: 255
Mode: 255
Median: 168.0

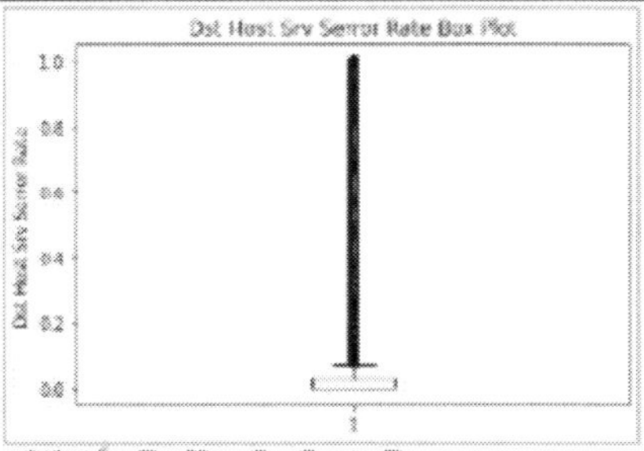

Statistics for Dst Host Srv Serror Rate
Standard deviation: 0.30626147385957214
Mean: 0.1322609119943222
Max: 1.0
Mode: 0.0
Median: 0.0

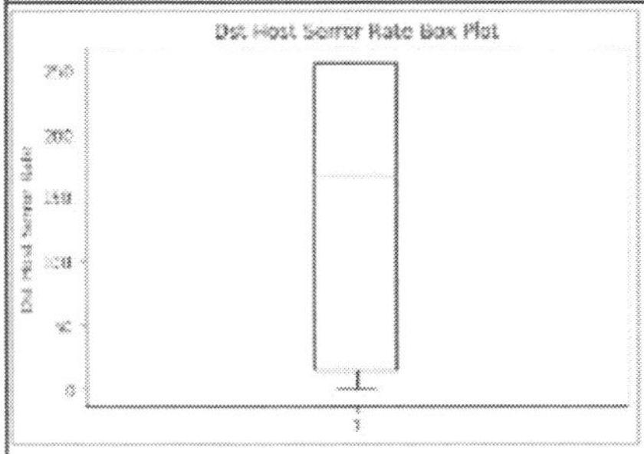

Statistics for Dst Host Serror Rate
Standard deviation: 111.78149290245192
Mean: 140.75053229240595
Max: 255
Mode: 255
Median: 168.0

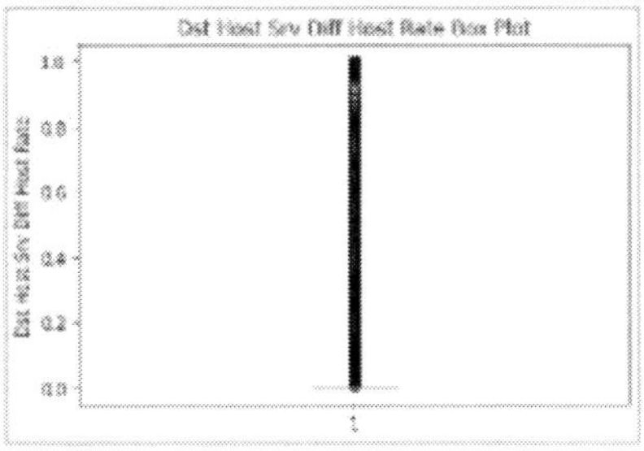

Statistics for Dst Host Srv Diff Host Rate
Standard deviation: 0.27313267988876393
Mean: 0.09781360894251243
Max: 1.0
Mode: 0.0
Median: 0.0

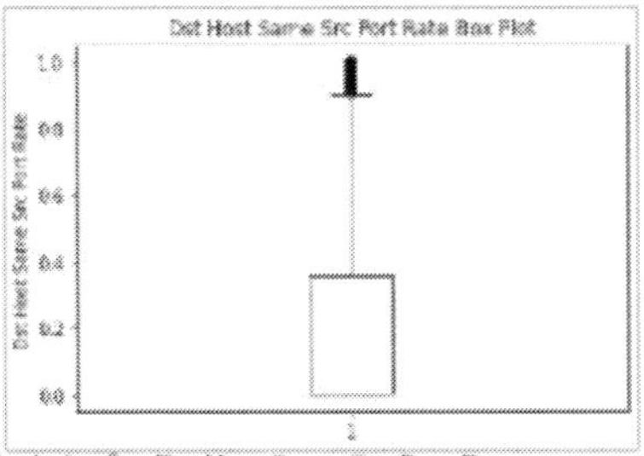

Statistics for Dst Host Same Src Port Rate
Standard deviation: 0.38722021628266123
Mean: 0.23338493612491126
Max: 1.0
Mode: 0.0
Median: 0.0

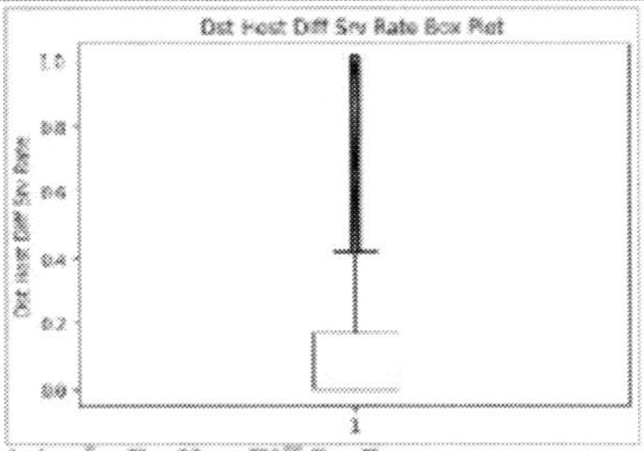

Statistics for Dst Host Diff Srv Rate
Standard deviation: 0.40086598668873476
Mean: 0.22668293115684884
Max: 1.0
Mode: 0.0
Median: 0.0

Figure 6.2: Box and Whisker Plot of NSI KDD Important Features Part2

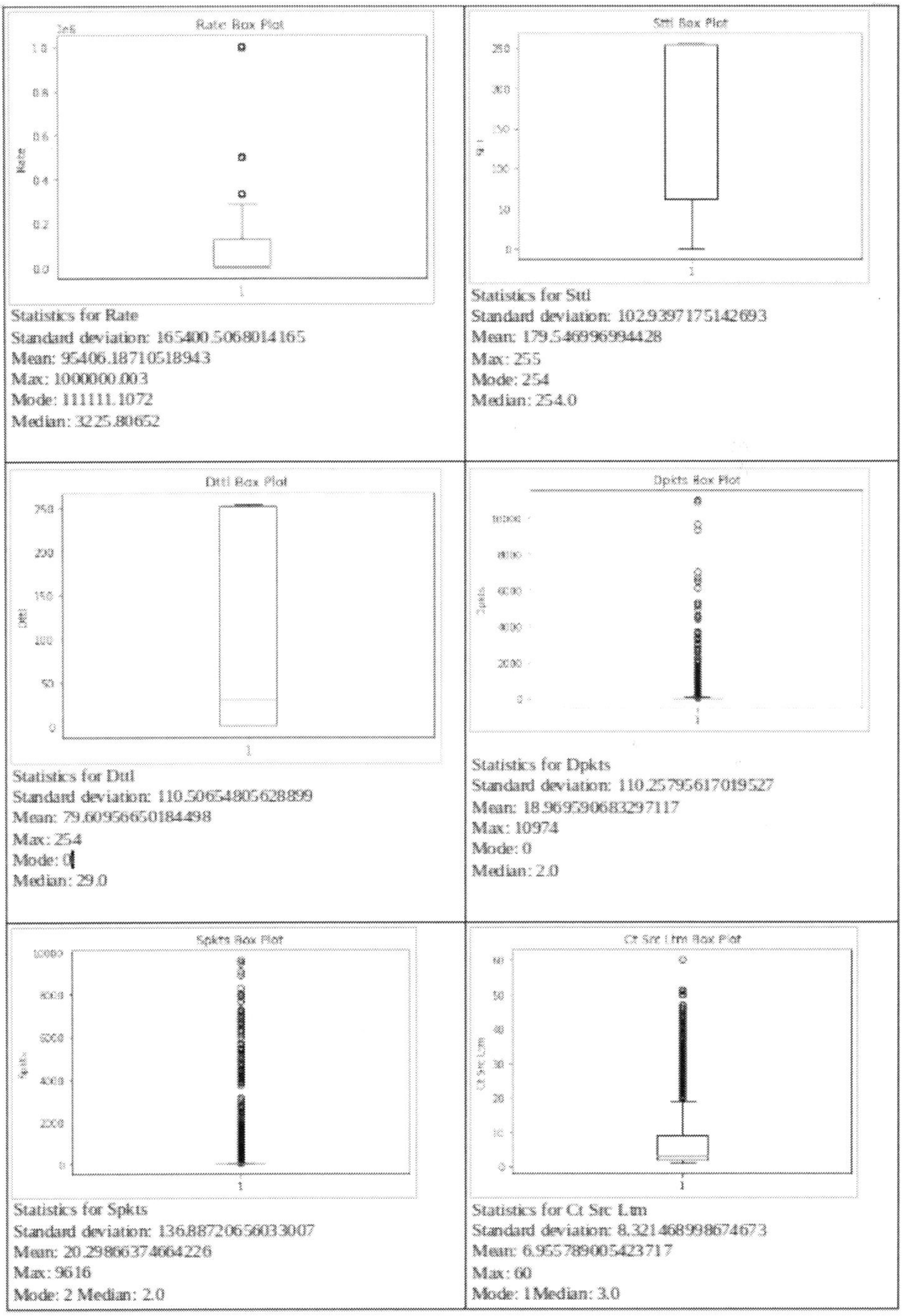

Figure 6.3: Box and Whisker Plot of UNSW NB 15 Important Features Part1

Figures 6.1a, 6.1b, which show how accurately attacks are detected. The x axis shows the number of epoch cycles, and the y axis shows accuracy. As shown in the graphs, accuracy rate increases as the number of epochs increases. Figures 6.2a, 6.2b, show the decrease in training and validation. The x axis shows the number of epoch cycles, whereas the y axis shows a loss. The graphs show the number of epochs, which are increasing, whereas training loss and validation are falling.

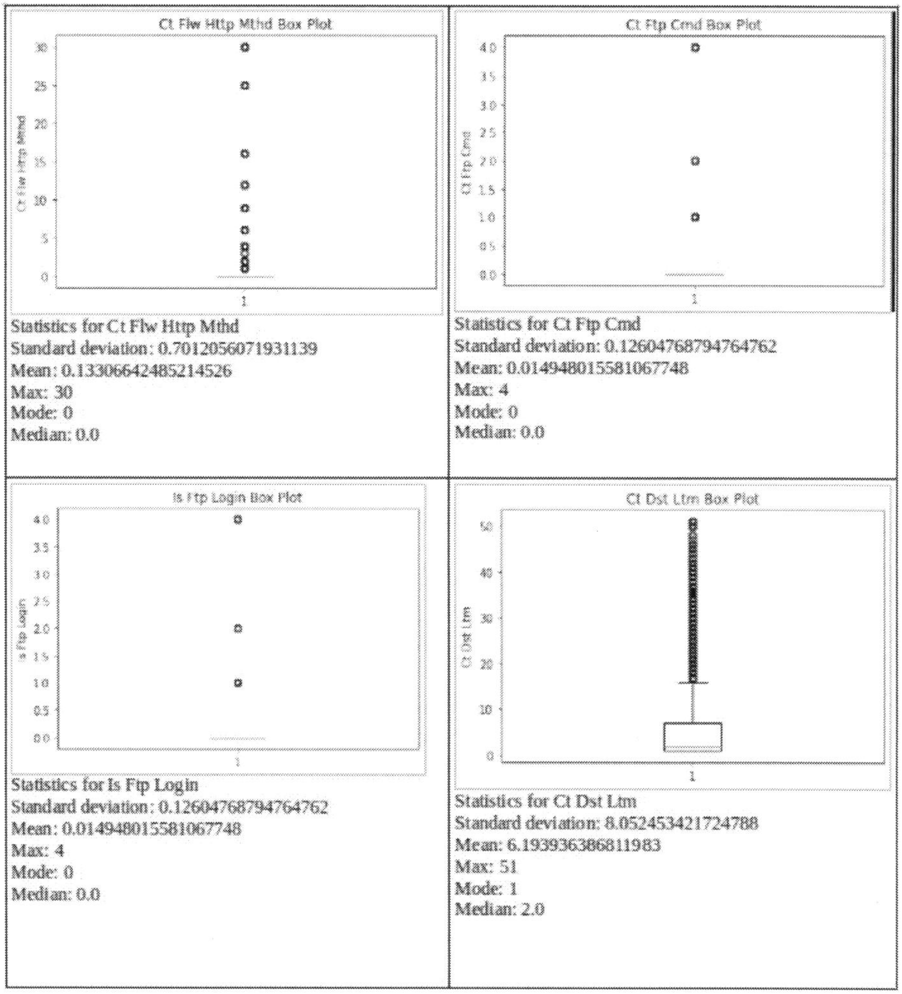

Figure 6.4: Box and Whisker Plot of UNSW NB 15 Important Features Part2

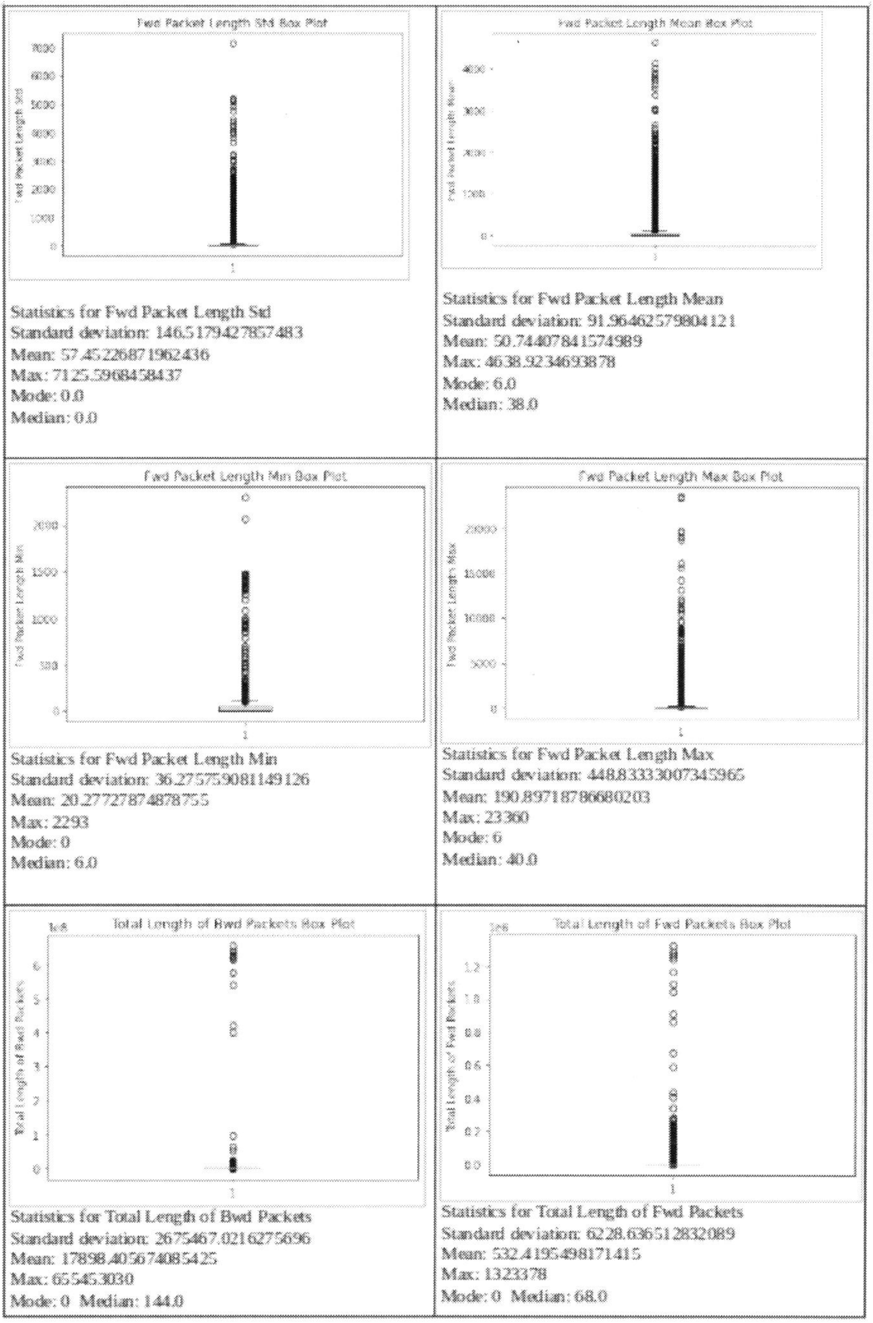

Statistics for Fwd Packet Length Std
Standard deviation: 146.5179427857483
Mean: 57.45226871962436
Max: 7125.5968458437
Mode: 0.0
Median: 0.0

Statistics for Fwd Packet Length Mean
Standard deviation: 91.96462579804121
Mean: 50.744078841574989
Max: 4638.92346938 78
Mode: 6.0
Median: 38.0

Statistics for Fwd Packet Length Min
Standard deviation: 36.27575908114912 6
Mean: 20.27727874878755
Max: 2293
Mode: 0
Median: 6.0

Statistics for Fwd Packet Length Max
Standard deviation: 448.8333300734596 5
Mean: 190.897187806802 03
Max: 23360
Mode: 6
Median: 40.0

Statistics for Total Length of Bwd Packets
Standard deviation: 2675467.0216275696
Mean: 17898.405674085425
Max: 655453030
Mode: 0 Median: 144.0

Statistics for Total Length of Fwd Packets
Standard deviation: 6228.636512832089
Mean: 532.4195498171415
Max: 1323378
Mode: 0 Median: 68.0

Figure 6.5: Box and Whisker Plot of CICIDS 2017 Important Features Part1

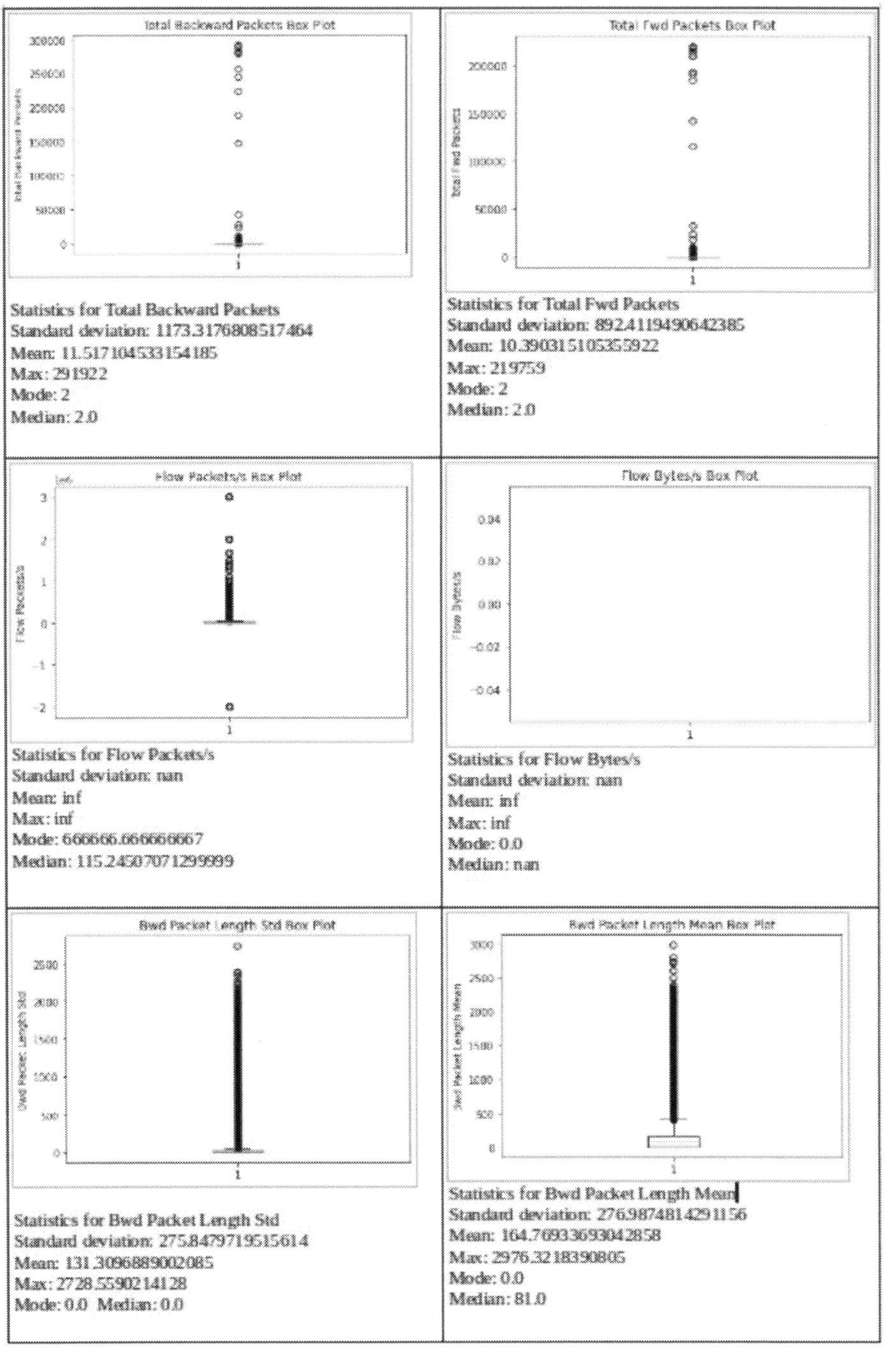

Figure 6.6: Box and Whisker Plot of CICIDS 2017 Important Features Part2

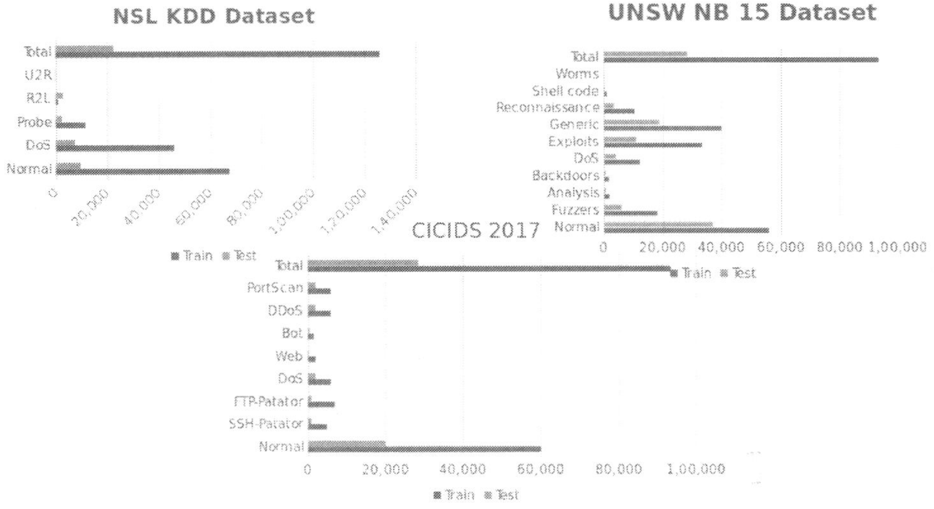

Figure 6.7: Attacks related information of all datasets

6.2.2 Confusion Matrix

Each column of the Confusion Matrix(cm) represents a predicted class, and each row represents an actual class. True Negative (TN) and False Positive (FP) are recorded for normal classes, whereas True Positive (TP) and False Negative (FN) are recorded for assault classes.

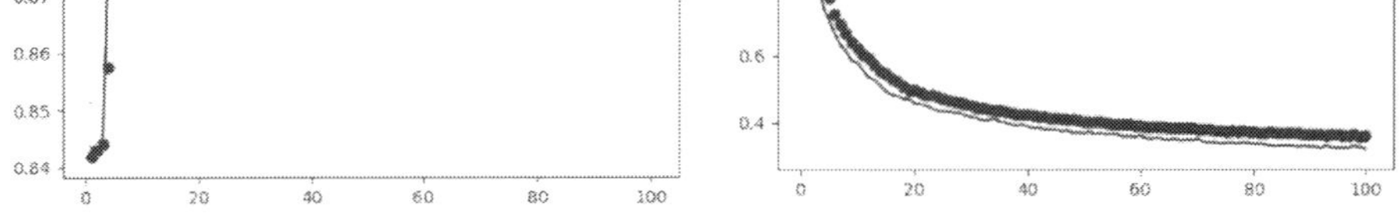

(a) CNN with LeeNet - Accuracy

(b) CNN with LeeNet - Loss

Figure 6.8: CNN LeeNet with NSL KDD Dataset

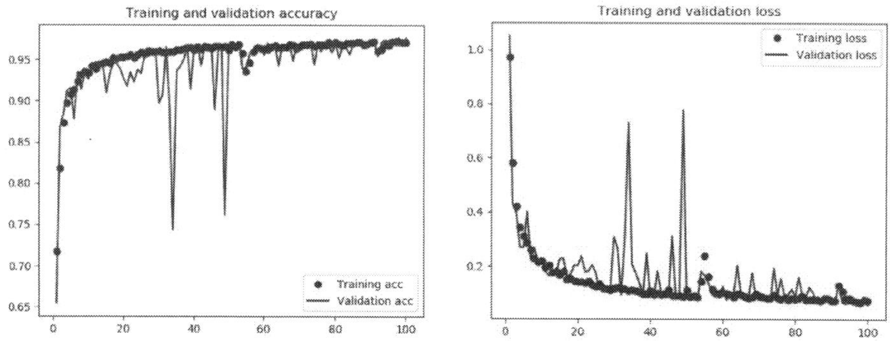

(a) CNN with ResNet - Accuracy (b) CNN with ResNet - Loss

Figure 6.9: CNN ResNet with NSL KDD Dataset

Confusion Matrix of the CICIDS2017 Dataset

Table 6.5 shows the CM of the classification for the CICIDS2017. With j = 5, the overall accuracy is 95.23% percent. The accuracy percentages for the different attack classes are 95.75 percent, 95.49 percent, 96.41 percent, and 93.21 percent, respectively. The low false negatives are also displayed in the first column. In addition, the assault classes have a small FPR (0.15 percent, 1.72 percent, 0.80 percent, and 2.15 percent, respectively).

Table 6.5: Confusion matrix of CICIDS 2017 dataset

Correct	Normal	DoS (Hulk)	DoS (Slowloris)	FTP	SSH
Normal	**5711 (95.37 %)**	9 (0.15%)	103 (1.72%)	48 (0.80%)	129 (2.15 %)
DoS (Hulk)	93 (1.55%)	**5745 (95.75%)**	33 (0.55%)	43 (0.72%)	86 (1.43%)
DoS (Slowloris)	107 (1.78%)	0 (0%)	**5718 (95.49%)**	93 (1.55%)	82 (1.37%)
FTP	43 (0.72%)	1 (0.02%)	127 (2.12%)	**5773 (96.41%)**	55 0.92%)
SSH	124 (2.07%)	34 (0.57%)	110 (1.84%)	150 (2.5%)	**5582 (93.21%)**

Confusion Matrix of the NSL KDD Dataset

Table 6.6 shows the CM of the classification for the NSL KDD dataset. With j = 5, the overall accuracy is 97.25% percent. The accuracy percentages for the different attack classes are 97.39 percent, 97.04 percent, 97.73 percent, and 97.43 percent, respectively. The low false negatives are also displayed in the first column. In addition, the assault classes have a small FPR (1.02 percent, 0.60 percent, 0.37 percent, and 1.47 percent, respectively).

Table 6.6: Confusion matrix of NSL KDD dataset

Correct	Normal	DoS	Probe	R2L	U2R
Normal	**5793 (96.74 %)**	61 (1.02 %)	36 (0.60 %)	22 (0.37%)	88 (1.47%)
DoS	92 (1.54 %)	**5832 (97.39%)**	53 (0.89%)	12 (0.2%)	11 (0.18%)
Probe	61 (1.12%)	55 (0.92%)	**5811 (97.04%)**	19 (0.32%)	44 (0.23%)
R2L	12 (0.2%)	7 (0.12%)	27 (0.45%)	**5852 (97.73%)**	102 (1.70%)
U2R	86 (1.43%)	6 (0.1%)	31 (0.52%)	43 (0.72%)	**5834 (97.43%)**

Confusion Matrix of the UNSW- NB 2015 Dataset

Table 6.7 shows the CM of the classification for the UNSW- NB 2015 dataset, the overall accuracy is 92.81% percent. The accuracy percentages for the different attack classes are 96.29 percent, 94 percent, 93.65 percent, and 92.66 percent, 94.88,92.91,91.42,90.21,86.37 respectively. The low false negatives are also displayed in the first column. In addition, the assault classes have a small FPR (0.32,0.34,0 .3,0.5,0.62,0.62,0.24,1.25,0.26, respectively).

Table 6.7: Confusion Matrix of UNSW NB 15 Dataset

Correct	Normal	Generic	Exploits	Fuzzers	DoS	Reconnaissance	Analysis	Backdoor	Shellcode	Worm
Normal	**35410 (95.7 %)**	118 (0.32 %)	124 (0.34%)	111 (0.3 %)	130 (0.35 %)	233 (0.62%)	230 (0.62 %)	90 (0.24%)	456 (1.23%)	98 (0.26%)
Generic	89 (0.47 %)	**18172 (96.29%)**	34 (0.18 %)	123 (0.65 %)	23 (0.12 %)	98 (0.51 %)	110 (0.58 %)	120 (0.64 %)	59 (0.31 %)	43 (0.22 %)
Exploits	123 (1.10 %)	47 (0.42 %)	**10465 (94 %)**	56 (0.50 %)	134 (1.20 %)	78 (0.7 %)	87 (0.78 %)	68 (0.61 %)	51 (0.46 %)	23 (0.21 %)
Fuzzer	71 (1.17 %)	27 (0.45 %)	46 (0.76 %)	**5677 93.65 %)**	35 (0.578%)	6 (0.098%)	23 (0.38 %)	34 (0.56 %)	56 (0.92 %)	87 (1.44 %)
DoS	34 (0.83 %)	45 (1.10 %)	22 (0.54 %)	78 (1.91 %)	**3789 (92.66 %)**	61 (1.49 %)	23 (0.56 %)	12 (0.29 %)	18 (0.44 %)	7 (0.17 %)

Correct	Normal	Generic	Exploits	Fuzzers	DoS	Reconnaissance	Analysis	Backdoor	Shell code	Worm
Reconnaissance	18 (0.51 %)	11 (0.31 %)	34 (0.97 %)	14 (0.40 %)	45 (1.29 %)	**3317 (94.88 %)**	45 (1.29 %)	4 (0.11 %)	1 (0.028 %)	7 (0.200%)
Analysis	13 (1.92 %)	13 (1.92 %)	4 (0.59 %)	6 (0.89 %)	7 (1.03 %)	2 (0.30 %)	**629 92.91 %)**	2 (0.29 %)	0	1 (0.14 %)
Backdoor	23 (3.95 %)	12 (2.05 %)	1 (0.17 %)	2 (0.34 %)	6 (1.02 %)	1 (0.17 %)	2 (0.4 %)	**533 91.42 %)**	2 (0.34 %)	1 (0.17 %)
Shell code	12 (3.17 %)	0	0	7 (1.85 %)	8 (2.12 %)	9 (2.38 %)	0	0	**341 (90.21 %)**	1 (0.26 %)
worm	2 (4.55 %)	0	0	0	1 (2.27 %)	1 (2.27 %)	0	0	2 (4.55 %)	**38 (86.37 %)**

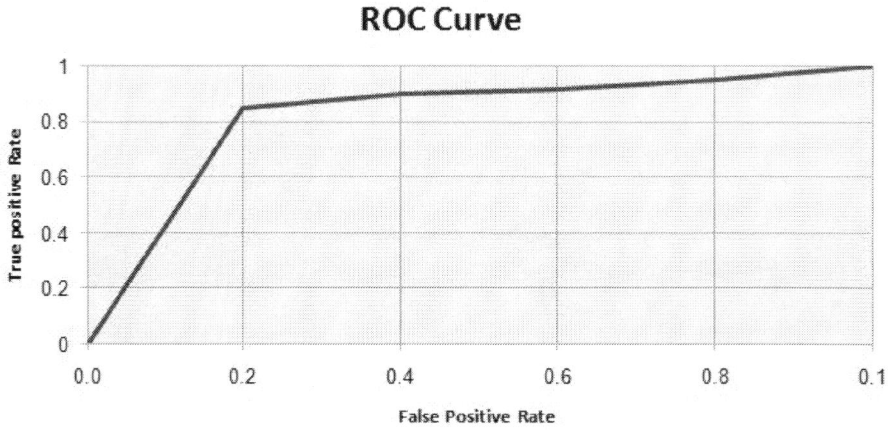

Figure 6.10: ROC of Final System

To measure and evaluate the model's overall accuracy, recall, precision, and F1 score, the ROC curve was utilised.

6.2.3 Result of Combined System

Experiment #4: Final system

The outcome of the combined signature-based and anomaly-based model is displayed below, and the chart and ROC curve of the suggested System, respectively, give result visualisation. First, the system will use the SIDS module to look for intrusions; when no intrusions are discovered, the system will next use the AIDS module to look for abnormalities; if any are found, an alarm will be generated, and a signature will be created. The following graph illustrates how integrating two systems increases accuracy.

Significant contribution is the design and implementation of an intelligent system that allows the System to learn from previous intrusion attempts and prepare rules.

Accuracy : 98.98%

Precision : 98%

F1- Score : 97%

Recall : 97 %

6.3 Summary of Result

This Table 6.8 shows the consolidated results all modules separately. The first stage Anomaly-based IDS system utilised Decision Tree to verify the attacks from the Signature Ruleset, while the second stage Anomaly-based IDS system used Deep learning method ResNet50 to check the attacks from the Signature Ruleset. Comparative analysis is also presented in the Figure 6.3, here 6.3a , 6.3b,6.3c are UNSW NB15 dataset, NSL-KDD Dataset and CICIDS 2017 dataset respectively.

Correct	Normal	DoS	Probe	R2L	U2R
Normal	**5793**	61	36	22	88
DoS	92	**5832**	53	12	11
Probe	61	55	**5811**	19	44
R2L	12	7	27	**5852**	102
U2R	86	6	31	43	**5834**

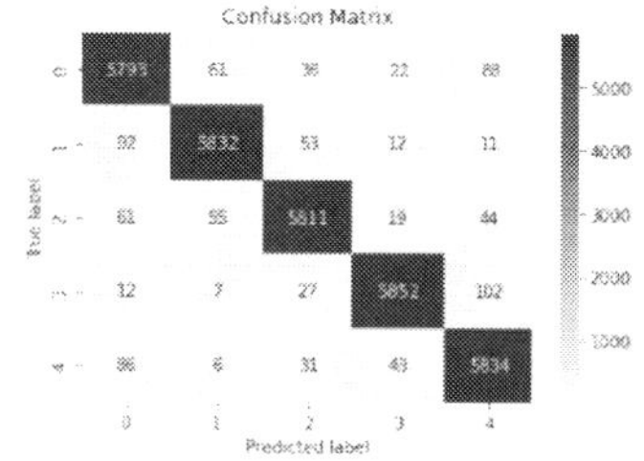

Figure 6.11: Confusion Matrix of NSL KDD dataset

Correct	Nor mal	Gene ric	Expl oits	Fuzzers	DoS	Reco nnais sance	Anal ysis	Back door	Sell code	Wor m
Normal	**35410**	118	124	111	130	233	230	90	456	98
Generic	89	**18172**	34	123	23	98	110	120	59	43
Exploits	123	47	**10465**	56	134	78	87	68	51	23
Fuzzer	71	27	46	**5677**	35	6	23	34	56	87
DoS	34	45	22	78	**3789**	61	23	12	18	7
Reconnai ssance	18	11	34	14	45	**3317**	45	4	1	7
Analysis	13	13	4	6	7	2	**629**	2	0	1
Backdoo r	23	12	1	2	6	1	2	**533**	2	1
Shell code	12	0	0	7	8	9	0	0	**341**	1
worm	2	0	0	0	1	1	0	0	2	**38**

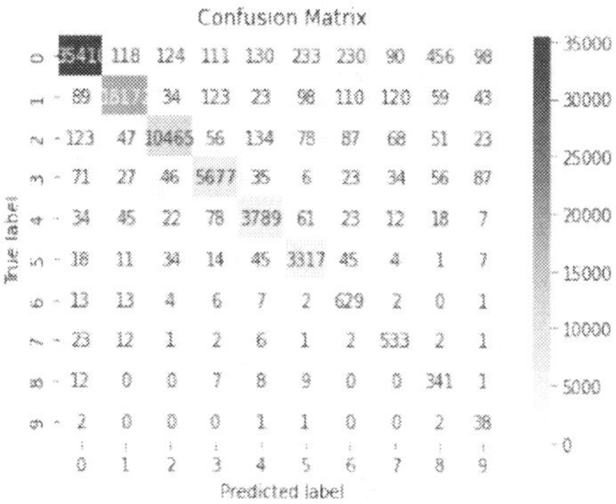

Figure 6.12: Confusion Matrix of UNSW NB 15 dataset

Figures 6.11, 6.12 and 6.13 gives confusion matrix of NSL-KDD Dataset, UNSW NB15 dataset and CICIDS 2017 dataset respectively. In figure 6.13, 6.14, 6.15 represents comparative analysis with LR: Linear Regression, NB- Naïve Bayes KNN- K Nearest Neighbor, DT-Decision Tree, AB- Ada Boost, RF- Random Forest, SVM- Support Vector Machine of same datasets.

Correct	Norm al	DoS Hulk	DoS (Slowloris)	FTP	SSH
Normal	**5711**	9	103	48	129
DoS Hulk	93	**5745**	33	43	86
DoS (Slowloris)	107	0	**5718**	93	82
FTP	43	1	127	**5773**	55
SSH	124	34	110	150	**5582**

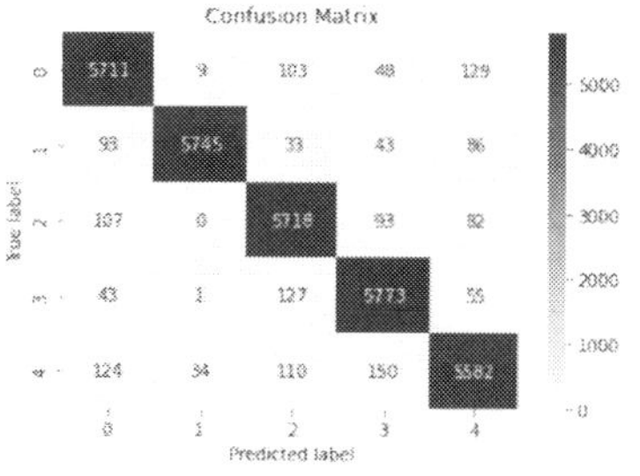

Figure 6.13: Confusion Matrix of CICIDS 2017 dataset

Algorithm	Accuracy	Precision	Recall	F-score
LR	0.612	0.509	0.612	0.530
NB	0.295	0.2907	0.295	0.184
KNN	0.731	0.720	0.731	0.684
DT	0.763	0.767	0.763	0.728
AB	0.621	0.651	0.621	0.594
RF	0.753	0.814	0.753	0.715
SVM	0.702	0.689	0.702	0.656
Proposed Model	**0.9725**	**0.98**	**0.92**	**0.95**

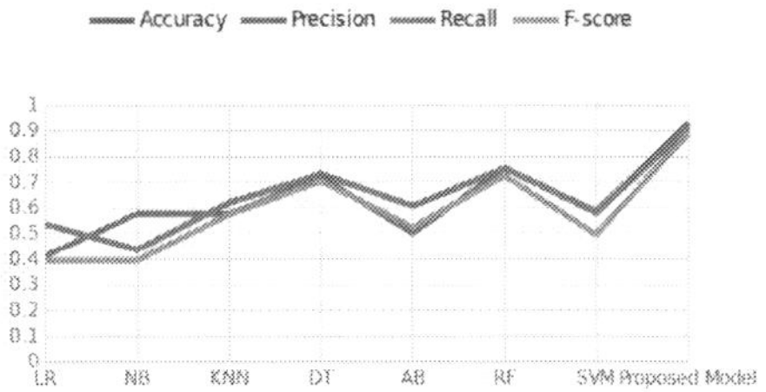

Figure 6.14: Comparative Analysis on NSL -KDD Datset

Algorithm	Accuracy	Precision	Recall	F-score
LR	0.870	0.889	0.870	0.868
NB	0.250	0.767	0.250	0.188
KNN	0.909	0.949	0.909	0.922
DT	0.940	0.965	0.940	0.949
AB	0.641	0.691	0.641	0.653
RF	0.944	0.970	0.944	0.953
SVM	0.799	0.757	0.799	0.723
Proposed Model	**0.9523**	**0.9563**	**0.9523**	**0.9492**

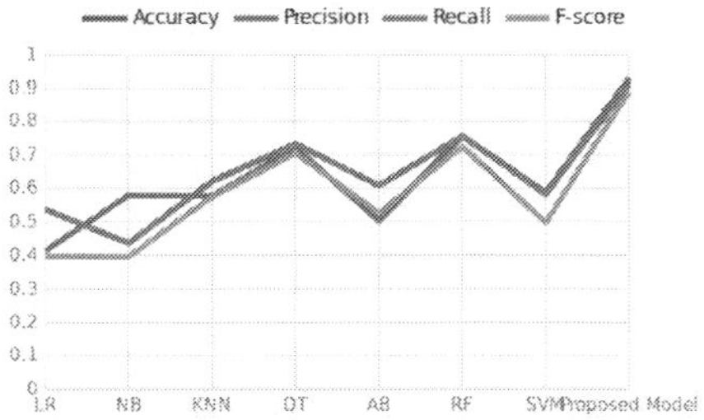

Figure 6.15: Comparative Analysis on CICIDS 2017 Datset

Algorithm	Accuracy	Precision	Recall	F-score
LR	0.538	0.414	0.538	0.397
NB	0.437	0.579	0.437	0.396
KNN	0.622	0.578	0.622	0.576
DT	0.733	0.721	0.733	0.705
AB	0.608	0.502	0.608	0.526
RF	0.755	0.755	0.755	0.724
SVM	0.581	0.586	0.581	0.496
Proposed Model	**0.9218**	**0.93**	**0.91**	**0.89**

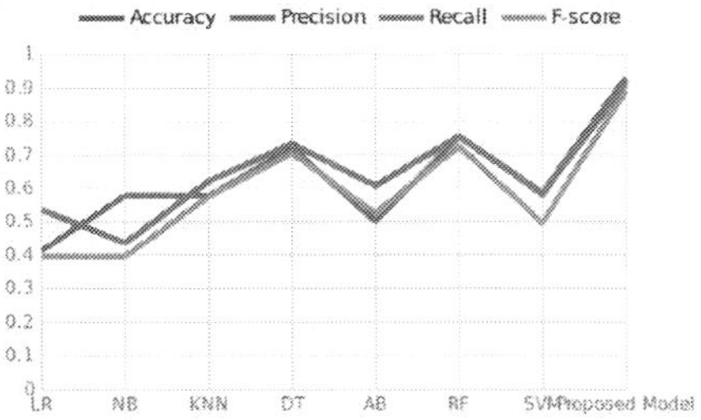

Figure 6.16: Comparative Analysis on UNSW NB 2015 Datset

Table 6.8: Consolidated Result of all modules of proposed system

System	Accuracy	Precision	Recall	F1- Score
Signature based IDS	96.6%	96%	95 %	95%
Anomaly Based IDS	97.25%	95%	98%	92%
Proposed System	98.98%	98%	96%	97%

The model is based on ResNet50, a 50-layer Convolutional Neural Network with a 97.25 percent accuracy rating. The third step detects known and unknown threats by categorising all network packets into normal and attack categories, and produces signatures using anomaly-based IDS. It has a detection accuracy of 98.98 percent for incursion. The suggested intrusion detection system is capable of detecting real-world intrusions successfully, according to our findings. ROC curve of final system is shown here in the Figure 6.10. The probability of false alarms and the probability of detection measurements are combined to form a receiver operating characteristic curve.

Table 6.9: Consolidated Result of all modules

Module	Technique	Learning technique	Dataset	Accuracy
Signature based IDS	Machine learning	Decision Tree	Snort Rule	96.96%
Anomaly Based IDS	Deep Learning	CNN with ResNet 50	NSL KDD, CICIDS 2017, UNSW NB-15	97.25%, 95.23%, 92.81%
Combined Approach	Machine Leaning+ Deep Learning	Decision Tree for SIDS ResNet 50 for AIDS with Signature Generation	Snort Rule Dataset and NSL KDD dataset	98.98 %

6.4 Testing Proposed System with Real Time Data

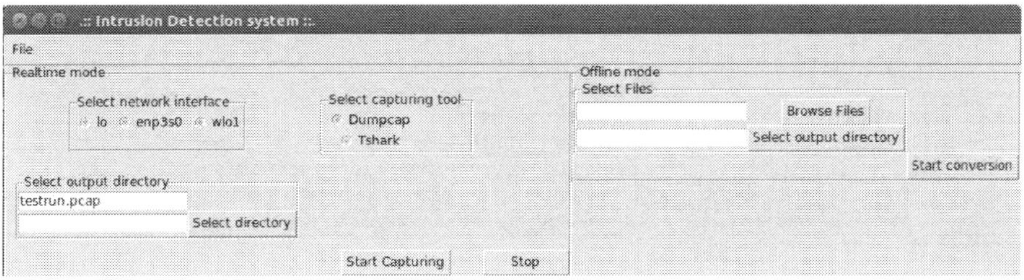

Figure 6.17: Intrusion Detection system for Network Interface

Testing of proposed system with real time data is done by real time capturing of packets from the institutional LAN network by selecting Network Interfaces as shown in Figure 6.5. A network interface is network-specific software that connects with the network-specific device driver and the IP layer to give a consistent interface to all network adapters. Standard Ethernet Version 2 (en), Loopback (lo), W01 as a wireless WIFI Router are used to connect Network with system. Here used Python's Scapy to sniff HTTP packets on the network throughout this data collecting procedure.Figure 6.6 shows continuous real time packet capturing. Here continue to sniff packets, and as they are received, this extract information from them [15], such as the source IP address, source port number, destination IP address,destination port, and so on. To analyse packets, this used the Python Scapy package because multiple network packets are supported, and classes are included to collect packets from various network segments and execute various actions with each one. It is shown in Module 1 how to retrieve packets from a network. The IP layer chooses the proper network interface depending on the packet's destination address. A network address is assigned to each network interface.Then preprocessing, feature extraction applied. Then this attack name and probabilities of detection in Figure 6.7. The enormous number of alarms produced by intrusion detection might be a major challenge. To reduce false alarm, in proposed system set threshold of 60% . So it will alert only if more than 60% probabilities matches with existing attack information. Then in Figure 6.8 alarm generation shown . If intrusion detected then extract the signature and add those into Ruleset shown in Figure 6.9.

Figure 6.18: Packet capture

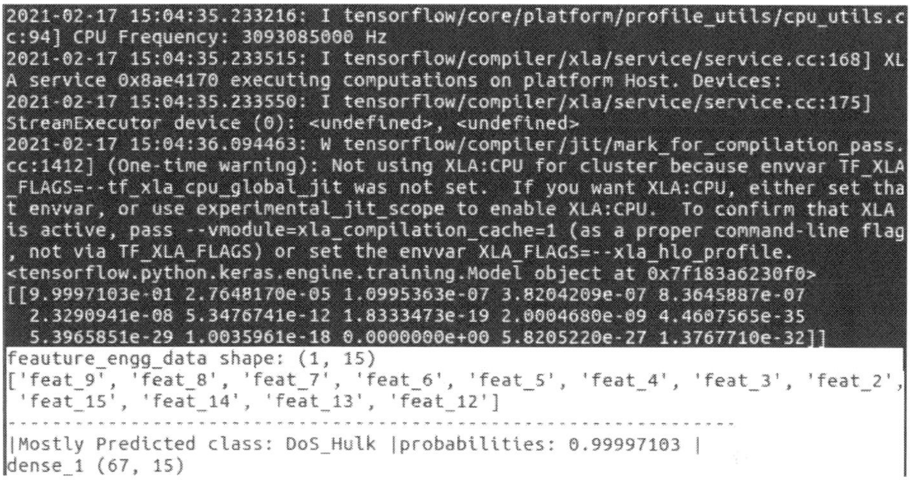

```
2021-02-17 15:04:35.233216: I tensorflow/core/platform/profile_utils/cpu_utils.c
c:94] CPU Frequency: 3093085000 Hz
2021-02-17 15:04:35.233515: I tensorflow/compiler/xla/service/service.cc:168] XL
A service 0x8ae4170 executing computations on platform Host. Devices:
2021-02-17 15:04:35.233550: I tensorflow/compiler/xla/service/service.cc:175]
StreamExecutor device (0): <undefined>, <undefined>
2021-02-17 15:04:36.094463: W tensorflow/compiler/jit/mark_for_compilation_pass.
cc:1412] (One-time warning): Not using XLA:CPU for cluster because envvar TF_XLA
_FLAGS=--tf_xla_cpu_global_jit was not set.  If you want XLA:CPU, either set tha
t envvar, or use experimental_jit_scope to enable XLA:CPU.  To confirm that XLA
is active, pass --vmodule=xla_compilation_cache=1 (as a proper command-line flag
, not via TF_XLA_FLAGS) or set the envvar XLA_FLAGS=--xla_hlo_profile.
<tensorflow.python.keras.engine.training.Model object at 0x7f183a6230f0>
[[9.9997103e-01 2.7648170e-05 1.0995363e-07 3.8204209e-07 8.3645887e-07
  2.3290941e-08 5.3476741e-12 1.8333473e-19 2.0004680e-09 4.4607565e-35
  5.3965851e-29 1.0035961e-18 0.0000000e+00 5.8205220e-27 1.3767710e-32]]
feauture_engg_data shape: (1, 15)
['feat_9', 'feat_8', 'feat_7', 'feat_6', 'feat_5', 'feat_4', 'feat_3', 'feat_2',
 'feat_15', 'feat_14', 'feat_13', 'feat_12']
-------------------------------------------------------------------
|Mostly Predicted class: DoS_Hulk |probabilities: 0.99997103 |
dense_1 (67, 15)
```

Figure 6.19: Attack details

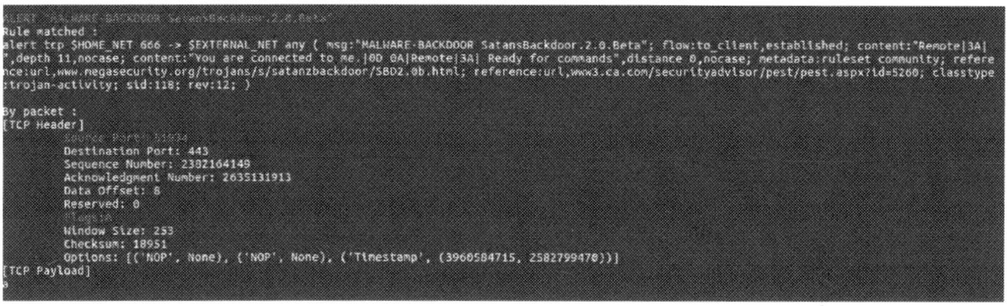

```
Rule matched :
alert tcp $HOME_NET 666 -> $EXTERNAL_NET any ( msg:"MALWARE-BACKDOOR SatansBackdoor.2.0.Beta"; flow:to_client,established; content:"Remote|3A|
",depth 11,nocase; content:"You are connected to me.|0D 0A|Remote|3A| Ready for commands",distance 0,nocase; metadata:ruleset community; refere
nce:url,www.megasecurity.org/trojans/s/satanzbackdoor/SBD2.0b.html; reference:url,www3.ca.com/securityadvisor/pest/pest.aspx?id=5260; classtype
:trojan-activity; sid:118; rev:12; )

By packet :
[TCP Header]
        Destination Port: 443
        Sequence Number: 2382164149
        Acknowledgment Number: 2635131913
        Data Offset: 8
        Reserved: 0
        Window Size: 253
        Checksum: 18951
        Options: [('NOP', None), ('NOP', None), ('Timestamp', (3960584715, 2582799470))]
[TCP Payload]
```

Figure 6.20: Alarm Generation

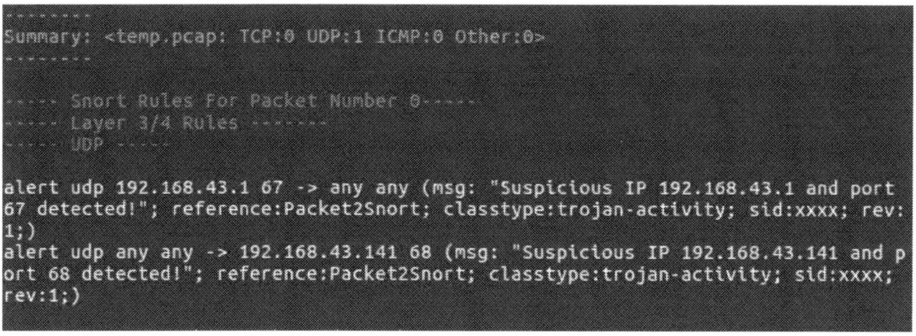

```
--------
Summary: <temp.pcap: TCP:0 UDP:1 ICMP:0 Other:0>
--------

----- Snort Rules For Packet Number 0-----
----- Layer 3/4 Rules -------
----- UDP -----

alert udp 192.168.43.1 67 -> any any (msg: "Suspicious IP 192.168.43.1 and port
67 detected!"; reference:Packet2Snort; classtype:trojan-activity; sid:xxxx; rev:
1;)
alert udp any any -> 192.168.43.141 68 (msg: "Suspicious IP 192.168.43.141 and p
ort 68 detected!"; reference:Packet2Snort; classtype:trojan-activity; sid:xxxx;
rev:1;)
```

Figure 6.21: Rules created

6.5 Analysis of Proposed System with Other Existing Techniques

The proposed system is compared with the existing work of various researchers based on algorithm used, learning techniques employed, different datasets used for testing and accuracy. Comparison shown in Table 6.10.

Table 6.10: Comparative analysis with existing techniques

Author Name	Year	Algorithm used	Learning technique	Dataset	Accuracy
W. Seo et al. [17]	2021	Deep learning	Two-level classifier	UNSW-NB15	95.8%
Duo, et al. [18]	2021	Deep learning	Genetic algorithm support vector machines (GA-SVM) and particle swarm optimisation	KDD-99	90.3% to 95.75
Devan P. Khare et.al.[21]	2020	Deep Learning	XGBoost–DNN model	NSL-KDD	98.91%
X. Li et al. [22]	2021	Machine learning	Multi-class regression models, long-term ensemble learning	NSL KDD	96.92%
F. Z. Belgrana et al. [24]	2021	Machine Learning	Condensed Nearest Neighbors (CoNN) algorithm	NSL-KDD	98.65%
H. Zhou,et.al.[30]	2020	Deep learning	Convolutional neural network (CNN) with automated Signature generation	NSL KDD	97.5%
K. Jiang et. al. [31]	2020	Deep Learning	CNN to pull out characteristics and a BiLSTM	NSL-KDD and UNSW-NB15 d	83.58% and 77.16%

Author Name	**Year**	**Algorithm used**	**Learning technique**	**Dataset**	**Accuracy**
M. Azizjon et al. [32]	2020	Deep Learning	Two-dimensional CNN	UNSWNB15	91.17%
Xiao et al.[39]	2019	Deep learning	CNN model of Lenet-5	KDD-CUP99	94%
Vinayakumar et al. [40]	2019	Deep learning	Deep neural network (DNN)	UNSW-NB15, NSL-KDD, WSN-DS, Kyoto, and CICIDS 2017	93.5%
X. Zhang et al. [42]	2019	Deep learning	CNN with SMOTE coupled with Edited Near	NSL KDD	83.31%.
Quamar Niyaz et al. [45]	2015	Deep learning	Self-taught Learning(STL)	NSL KDD	98%
S. Park et al. [69]	2018	Deep learning	convolutional autoencoder (CAE) and character-level binary image modification	MNIST dataset	98%
Bouyeddou et al. [66]	2020	Machine learning	Continuous Graded Probability Score (CRPS)	DARPA99, MAWI and ICMPv6	96% and 98%
Nathan Shone, et.al.[67]	2018	Deep learning	Non-symmetric deep auto-encoder (NDAE)	NSL-KDD and KDD Cup '99	97.85%

Author Name	Year	Algorithm used	Learning technique	Dataset	Accuracy
Ajith Abraham [70]	2017	Machine learning	Linear genetic programming , Decision trees and support vector machines	NSL KDD	94.65%
J. Jabez et. al.[76]	2018	Machine learning	Neighborhood Outlier Factor (NOF)	KDD 99	-
Hussein, S. M. [80]	2016	Machine learning	Naïve WEKA methods include Bayes, K-means, Bayes Net with Snort	KDD Cup 99	97.40%
Kruegel C [108]	2003	Machine Learning	Decision Tree	NSL KDD	95.68
Ansam Khraisat, et.al. [117]	2020	Machine learning	One Class Support Vector Machine and C5.0 Decision Tree Classifier	NSL-KDD and ADFA Dataset	83.24%
Proposed System	**2022**	**Machine Leaning+ Deep Learning**	**Decision Tree for SIDS and ResNet 50 for AIDS with Signature Generation**	**Snort Rule Dataset and NSL KDD dataset**	**98.98%**

6.6 Computational Complexity

6.6.1 Time Complexity

ResNet-50 CNN model

The time complexity of the ResNet-50 CNN model can be expressed as follows using Big-O notation:

$$O(kN^2L) \quad (6.5)$$

where k is the number of filters in each convolutional layer, N is the No of size of packet, and L is the number of layers in the network.

In ResNet-50, $k = 64$ and $L = 50$, and the input packet are 224×224, so the time complexity of ResNet-50 can be approximated as:

$$O(64 \times 224^2 \times 50) \approx O(1.6 \times 10^9) \quad (6.6)$$

This means that the ResNet-50 model takes roughly 1.6 billion operations.

Decision Tree

The time complexity of a decision tree algorithm depends on the number of training instances n, the number of features in the data m, and log m is the depth of the tree.In general, the time complexity of building a decision tree is proportional to the product of these factors, and can be expressed as follows using Big-O notation:

$$O(n * m * \log m), \quad (6.7)$$

Combined Approach

The time complexity of a neural network with a decision tree in the first layer and a ResNet-50 CNN model in the second layer can be expressed as the sum of the time complexities of each component. Let's assume that the decision tree has a depth of d_1 and the ResNet-50 model has L layers, and that the input packets to the ResNet-50 model have size $N \times N$.

The time complexity of the decision tree is given by:

$$O(nmd_1 \log n) \quad (6.8)$$

where n is the number of training instances, and m is the number of features in the data. The time complexity of the ResNet-50 model can be expressed as:

$$O(kN^2L) \quad (6.9)$$

where k is the number of filters in each convolutional layer.

As the output of the decision tree is fed as input to the ResNet-50 model, the total time complexity of the combined model can be expressed as:

$$O(nmd_1 \log n + kN L) \quad (6.10)$$

Note that the time complexity of the decision tree and the ResNet-50 model are independent of each other, so we simply add them up to get the total time complexity.

6.6.2 Space Complexity

The space complexity of the ResNet 50 CNN model refers to the amount of memory required to store the model's parameters, intermediate activations, and gradients during training and inference. The space complexity of ResNet 50 depends on several factors, including the number of layers, the size of each layer, the number of filters, and the size of the input data. In general, the space complexity of ResNet 50 can be expressed as:

$$Totalspace = Modelspace + Inputspace + Activationspace + Gradientspace \quad (6.11)$$

- **Model space:** This refers to the amount of memory required to store the parameters of the model, including the weights and biases for each layer. ResNet 50 has a total of approximately 25 million parameters, which results in a significant model space requirement.
- **Input space:** This refers to the amount of memory required to store the input data and any additional pre-processing steps. The input space is proportional to the size of the input data.
- **Activation space:** This refers to the amount of memory required to store the intermediate activations of the model during the forward pass. The activation space is proportional to the number of layers, the size of each layer, and the batch size. In ResNet 50, the largest activation space is required by the fully connected layer, which has 2048 units.
- **Gradient space:** This refers to the amount of memory required to store the gradients of the loss function with respect to the model parameters during the backward pass. The gradient space is proportional to the number of layers, the size of each layer, and the batch size.

Overall, the space complexity of ResNet 50 is high due to the large number of parameters and layers in the model. Therefore, running ResNet 50 on limited memory devices may require careful memory management, such as using smaller batch sizes or optimizing the implementation of the model.

Number of Binary Operations (BOP)

The number of binary operations (BOP) for a 1D-convolutional layer in a CNN can be calculated as follows:

To compute each element of the output tensor, we need to perform k multiplications and (k-1) additions for each position of the kernel sliding over the input. Since the kernel slides (input length - kernel size) / s + 1 positions over the input, the total number of BOP for the convolutional layer is:

$$BOP = batch\ size \times output\ length \times k \times kernel\ size \times input\ channels \times 2 \quad (6.12)$$

Here, we multiply by 2 because each multiplication and addition operation involves 2 binary operations (one for the multiply and one for the addition)

Number of MAC operations

The ResNet-50 model have size $N \times N$. The number of MAC operations in a convolutional layer with k filters and a kernel size of 3 × 3 can be approximated as $k \times N^2 \times 9$, since there are k filters, and each filter performs a 3 × 3 convolution on an $N \times N$ input. The number of MAC operations in a fully connected layer with n neurons can be approximated as $n \times c$, where c is the size of the input to the layer.

We can calculate the approximate number of MAC operations in each layer of the ResNet-50 model, and then sum them up to get the total number of MAC operations. The ResNet-50 model has 49 convolutional layers and 1 fully connected layer, so the total number of MAC operations can be approximated as:

$$\sum_{i=1}^{49} k_i \times N^2 \times 9 + 2048 \times 2048 + 2048 \times 1000 \quad (6.13)$$

where k_i is the number of filters in the i-th convolutional layer, and we have added the MAC operations in the final fully connected layer with 2048 neurons and the output layer with 1000 neurons.

In ResNet-50, $k_i = 64$ for all convolutional layers, so the total number of MAC operations can be approximated as:

$$\approx 64 \times N^2 \times 9 \times 49 + 2048 \times 2048 + 2048 \times 1000 \quad (6.14)$$

Decision trees are not based on MAC operations. They use a different approach for making predictions that does not involve multiply-accumulate operations like in convolutional neural networks.

6.7 Conclusion

Proposed intelligent Intrusion Detection System capable of detecting well known as well as zero-day attacks with higher accuracy with less false alarm rate. This proposed system includes enhanced security measures which detect known as well as known attacks to encourage the development of systems management applications and software-based frameworks to combat digital threats. Also an important contribution is the design and implementation of an intelligent system that allows the system to learn from previous intrusion attempts and prepare rules.

7

Conclusion

7.1 Conclusion

This research work design and develops a novel IDS approach by combining Signature and Anomaly based IDS approaches using the well-known NSL KDD dataset, CICIDS 2017 dataset, and UNSW 2015 dataset. The supplied IDS is designed with two detection engines, the first of which is based on a Decision Tree for signature-based IDS, and the second of which is based on the CNN ResNet 50 network for anomaly-based IDS, which is highly useful in cyber security research. Our recommended IDS, a three-stage learning process, also creates signatures from the anomaly observed and has a high prediction accuracy at the classification method level, with a predictive accuracy of 98.98 percent. The proposed combined IDS based on the Decision Tree and CNN ResNet50 network integrates the power of both, the Decision Tree and the CNN ResNet50 networks, which may be considered an efficient solution. Our IDS's hierarchical style not only outperforms advanced IDS approaches in terms of intrusion detection accuracy and reducing false alarms. It's also tested against real-time traffic from the local area network. The main findings and contributions of the proposed work can be summarized as follows:

- A detailed survey of the literature on IDS throughout the previous decade. The research looks at the most often used IDS datasets in the literature, as well as the machine learning and deep learning techniques used to build IDS and the cyber threats covered/detected. This book addresses shortcomings in present IDS and research requirements. To further analyse the cyber attacks covered by IDS, an expandable cyber threat taxonomy is provided.

- Proposed intrusion detection system capable of detecting a broad variety of attacks with a high detection rate and a low false alarm rate.
- Solved the imbalanced classifications problem by calculating the class weight of each features in the detail, so minority class also get correct detection.
- Proposed system include first detection engine - signature based analysis for intrusion detection system using decision tree here got accuracy of 96.96%.
- Proposed system include first detection engine for anomalies detection for anomaly based IDS using deep learning model ResNet 50 with adding class weights and activation modification and got accuracy of 97.25% , 95.23%, 92.18% using NSL KDD Dataset, CICIDS 2017, UNSW2015 respectively. Result of proposed system has given better result as compared with other research works mentioned in the literature survey
- After combining both Signature and Anomaly based Intrusion Detection System , also evaluate the performance and results received 98.98%. It is better result as compared with existing work.
- The quality of an IDS's signature ruleset is directly proportional to the strength of the IDS itself. As long as it isn't regularly updated, it won't be able to keep up with the most recent threats. Proposed system is very intelligent which allows the system to learn from previous intrusion attempts prepare rule and update into SIDS ruleset.
- Since cyberattacks are becoming more complex, it is getting harder to reliably identify breaches. This proposed IDS can be used in various areas to protect network from cyber attacks, automatic Evidence collection for Digital Forensic, etc.

7.2 Limitation

An intrusion detection system's performance get affected by noise. The false-alarm rate increases by bad packets created by software faults, faulty DNS data, and local packets that have escaped.

An IDS can read IP packet information, but the network address may still be faked. Using a bogus address makes it more difficult to identify and evaluate an attacker's danger.

To get into the network, an attacker may utilise encrypted packets to do so. This proposed IDS can't look through encrypted packets.

7.3 Future Enhancement

As future enhancement to the work the proposed intrusion detection system may be expanded to include intrusion prevention capability for making the entire environment more robust and less attack prone. Further we can test the proficiency of our model with IOT devices, clouds and mobile infrastructure, and wireless sensor networks.

Intrusion detection is an ever evolving process in this contemporary internet age as new attack types and variations on existing attacks are frequent. Alternate detection strategies may be tried in the future to deal with same.

The proposed existing system does not consider encrypted packets. The system can be appropriately modified for dealing with packets that are encrypted by the attacker.

Bibliography

[1] Herve Debar, Marc Dacier, Andreas Wespi, "Towards a taxonomy of intrusion-detection systems", 1999

[2] K. Scarfone, P. Mell, "Guide to Intrusion Detection and Prevention Systems (IDPS)," NIST Special Publication 800-94, Feb. 2007.

[3] Cisco Annual Internet Report—Cisco Annual Internet Report (2018–2023) White Paper—Cisco. [Online]. Available: https://www.cisco.com/c/en/us/solutions/collateral/executiveperspectives/annual-internet-report/white-paper-c11-741490.html

[4] Massive Brute-Force Attack on Alibaba Affects Millions. [Online]. Available: https://www.infosecurity-magazine.com/news/massive-bruteforce-attack-on(Oct. 2016). Dyn Analysis Summary of Friday October 21 Attack. [Online]. Available: https://web.archive.org/web/20200620203923/ and https://dyn.com/blog/ dyn-analysis-summary-of-friday-october-21-attack/

[5] Rani, M., Gagandeep Effective network intrusion detection by addressing class imbalance with deep neural networks multimedia tools and applications. Multimed Tools Appl (2022). https://doi.org/10.1007/s11042-021-11747-6

[6] Jing Yu, Xiaojun Ye, Hongbo Li, A high precision intrusion detection system for network security communication based on multi-scale convolutional neural network, Future Generation Computer Systems, Volume 129, 2022, Pages 399-406, ISSN 0167-739X, https://doi.org/10.1016/j.future.2021.10.018

[7] Wei Wang, Songlei Jian, Yusong Tan, Qingbo Wu, Chenlin Huang, Representation learning-based network intrusion detection system by capturing explicit and implicit feature interactions, Computers Security, Volume 112, 2022, 102537, ISSN 0167-4048, https://doi.org/10.1016/j.cose.2021.102537.

[8] R. V. Mendon¸ca et al., "Intrusion Detection System Based on Fast Hierarchical Deep Convolutional Neural Network," in

IEEE Access, vol. 9, pp. 61024-61034, 2021, doi: 10.1109/ACCESS.2021.3074664.

[9] A Shaikh, Kamatchi Iyer, Security and Privacy Issues in Cloud Computing. In: Hemanth J., Fernando X., Lafata P., Baig Z. (eds) International Conference on Intelligent Data Communication Technologies and Internet of Things (ICICI) 2018. ICICI 2018. Lecture Notes on Data Engineering and Communications Technologies, vol 26. Springer, Cham. https://doi.org/10.1007/978-3-030-03146-6 152

[10] A Shaikh, Sita Devulapalli, Intrusion Detection System : A survey", International Journal of Emerging Technologies and Innovative Research (www.jetir.org — UGC and issn Approved), ISSN:2349-5162, Vol.6, Issue 6, page no. pp440-446, June-2019

[11] A Shaikh, Sita Devulapalli, Proposed Deep learning method for Intrusion Detection System using LeeNet, International Journal of Advanced Research in Engineering and Technology (IJARET), 11(6), 2020, pp. 1202-1209.

[12] A Shaikh, Preeti Gupta, Real-time intrusion detection based on residual learning through ResNet algorithm. Int J Syst Assur Eng Manag (2022). https://doi.org/10.1007/s13198-021-01558-1

[13] A Shaikh, Preeti Gupta, Anomaly Based Intrusion Detection System Using Deep Learning Methods, Proceedings of the International Conference on Recent Advances in Computational Techniques (IC-RACT) 2020.

[14] A Shaikh, Preeti Gupta, Dynamic Updating of Signatures for Improving the Performance of Intrusion Detection System in 2 International Conference on Expert Clouds and Applications (ICOECA 2022), will published in Springer "Lecture Notes in Networks and Systems - 3rd and 4th Feb 2022

[15] Shaikh, A., Gupta, P.,Advanced Signature-Based Intrusion Detection System. In: Rajakumar, G., Du, KL., Vuppalapati, C., Beligiannis, G.N. (eds) Intelligent Communication Technologies and Virtual Mobile Networks. Lecture Notes on Data Engineering and Communications Technologies, vol 131. Springer, Singapore. https://doi.org/10.1007/978-981-19-1844-5 24

[16] K. Kendall, "A database of computer attacks for the evaluation of intrusion detection systems." Bachelor of Science, Electrical Engineering and Computer Science, 1999.

[17] W. Seo and W. Pak, "Real-Time Network Intrusion Prevention System Based on Hybrid Machine Learning," in IEEE Access, vol. 9, pp. 46386-46397, 2021, doi: 10.1109/ACCESS.2021.3066620.

[18] R. Duo, X. Nie, N. Yang, C. Yue and Y. Wang, "Anomaly Detection and Attack Classification for Train Real-Time Ethernet," in IEEE Access, vol. 9, pp. 22528-22541, 2021, doi: 10.1109/ACCESS.2021.3055209.

[19] S. Ho, S. A. Jufout, K. Dajani and M. Mozumdar, "A Novel Intrusion Detection Model for Detecting Known and Innovative Cyberattacks Using Convolutional Neural Network," in IEEE Open Journal of the Computer Society, vol. 2, pp. 14-25, 2021, doi: 10.1109/OJCS.2021.3050917.

[20] Jiarui Man, Guozi Sun, "A Residual Learning-Based Network Intrusion Detection System", Security and Communication Networks, vol. 2021, Article ID 5593435, 9 pages, 2021. https://doi.org/10.1155/2021/5593435

[21] Devan, P., Khare, N. An efficient XGBoost–DNN-based classification model for network intrusion detection system. Neural ComputApplic 32, 12499–12514 (2020).https://doi.org/10.1007/s00521-020-04708-x

[22] X. Li et al., "Sustainable Ensemble Learning Driving Intrusion Detection Model," in IEEE Transactions on Dependable and Secure Computing, doi: 10.1109/TDSC.2021.3066202.

[23] M. H. Haghighat and J. Li, "Intrusion detection system using voting-based neural network," in Tsinghua Science and Technology, vol. 26, no. 4, pp. 484-495, Aug. 2021, doi: 10.26599/TST.2020.9010022.

[24] F. Z. Belgrana, N. Benamrane, M. A. Hamaida, A. Mohamed Chaabani and A. Taleb-Ahmed, "Network Intrusion Detection System Using Neural Network and Condensed Nearest Neighbors with Selection of NSL-KDD Influencing Features," 2020 IEEE International Conference on Internet of Things and Intelligence System (IoTaIS), BALI, Indonesia, 2021, pp. 23-29, doi: 10.1109/IoTaIS50849.2021.9359689

[25] Karatas G, Demir O, Sahingoz OK. Increasing the performance of machine learning-based IDSs on an imbalanced and up-to-date dataset. IEEE Access. 2020;8:32150-32162. https://doi.org/10.1109/ACCESS.2020.2973219.

[26] Yang Y, Zheng K, Wu B, Yang Y, Wang X. Network intrusion detection based on supervised adversarial variational auto-

encoder with regularization. IEEE Access. 2020;8:42169-42184. https://doi.org/10.1109/ACCESS.2020.2977007.

[27] Phurivit Sangkatsanee, Naruemon Wattanapongsakorn, Chalermpol Charnsripinyo, Practical real-time intrusion detection using machine learning approaches, Computer Communications, Volume 34, Issue 18, 2011, Pages 2227-2235, ISSN 0140-3664, https://doi.org/10.1016/j.comcom.2011.07.001

[28] Yu Y, Bian N. An intrusion detection method using few-shot learning. IEEE Access. 2020;8:49730-49740. https://doi.org/10.1109/ACCESS. 2020.2980136.

[29] Andresini G, Appice A, Di Mauro N, Loglisci C, Malerba D. Multi-channel deep feature learning for intrusion detection. IEEE Access. 2020;8:53346-53359. https://doi.org/10.1109/ACCESS.2020.2980937.

[30] H. Zhou, Y. Hu, X. Yang, H. Pan, W. Guo and C. C. Zou, "A Worm Detection System Based on Deep Learning," in IEEE Access, vol. 8, pp. 205444-205454, 2020, doi: 10.1109/ACCESS.2020.3023434.

[31] K. Jiang, W. Wang, A. Wang and H. Wu, "Network Intrusion Detection Combined Hybrid Sampling With Deep Hierarchical Network," in IEEE Access, vol. 8, pp. 32464-32476, 2020, doi: 10.1109/ACCESS.2020.2973730.

[32] M. Azizjon, A. Jumabek and W. Kim, "1D CNN based network intrusion detection with normalization on imbalanced data," 2020 International Conference on Artificial Intelligence in Information and Communication (ICAIIC), Fukuoka, Japan, 2020, pp. 218-224, doi: 10.1109/ICAIIC48513.2020.9064976.

[33] R. Vinayakumar, M. Alazab, K. P. Soman, P. Poornachandran, A. Al-Nemrat and S. Venkatraman, "Deep Learning Approach for Intelligent Intrusion Detection System," in IEEE Access, vol. 7, pp. 41525-41550, 2019

[34] Y. Xiao, C. Xing, T. Zhang and Z. Zhao, "An Intrusion Detection Model Based on Feature Reduction and Convolutional Neural Networks," in IEEE Access, vol. 7, pp. 42210-42219, 2019, doi: 10.1109/ACCESS.2019.2904620.

[35] P. Wu and H. Guo, "LuNet: A Deep Neural Network for Network Intrusion Detection," 2019 IEEE Symposium Series on Computational Intelligence (SSCI), Xiamen, China, 2019, pp. 617-624, doi: 10.1109/SSCI44817.2019.9003126.

[36] X. Zhang, J. Ran and J. Mi, "An Intrusion Detection System Based on Convolutional Neural Network for Imbalanced Network Traffic," 2019 IEEE 7th International Conference on Computer Science and Network Technology (ICCSNT), Dalian, China, 2019, pp. 456-460, doi: 10.1109/ICCSNT47585.2019.8962490.

[37] Papamartzivanos D, M´armol FG, Kambourakis G. Introducing deep learning self-adaptive misuse network intrusion detection systems. IEEE Access. 2019;7:13546-13560. https://doi.org/10.1109/ACCESS.2019.2893871.

[38] Khan FA, Gumaei A, Derhab A, hussain A. A novel two-stage deep learning model for efficient network intrusion detection. IEEE Access. 2019;7:30373-30385. https://doi.org/10.1109/ACCESS.2019.2899721.

[39] Xiao Y, Xing C, Zhang T, Zhao Z. An intrusion detection model based on feature reduction and convolutional neural networks. IEEE Access. 2019;7:42210-42219. https://doi.org/10.1109/ACCESS.2019.2904620.

[40] Vinayakumar R, Alazab M, Soman K, Poornachandran P, Al-Nemrat A, Venkatraman S. Deep learning approach for intelligent intrusion detection system. IEEE Access. 2019;7:41525-41550. https://doi.org/10.1109/ACCESS.2019.2895334.

[41] Wei P, Li Y, Zhang Z, hu T, Li Z, Liu D. An optimization method for intrusion detection classification model based on deep belief network. IEEE Access. 2019;7:87593-87605. https://doi.org/10.1109/ACCESS.2019.2925828.

[42] Zhang X, Chen J, Zhou Y, han L, Lin J. A multiple-layer representation learning model for network-based attack detection. IEEE Access. 2019;7:91992-92008. https://doi.org/10.1109/ACCESS.2019.2927465.

[43] Kunal and Mohit Dua "Machine Learning Approach to IDS: A Comprehensive Review" Proceedings of the Third IEEE Conference Record 45616,2019

[44] Malaiya RK, Kwon D, Suh SC, Kim h, Kim I, Kim J. An empirical evaluation of deep learning for network anomaly detection. IEEE Access. 2019;7:140806-140817. https://doi.org/10.1109/ACCESS.2019.2943249.

[45] Quamar Niyaz, Ahmad Y Javaid, WeiqingSun and Mansoor Alam, 2015 "A Deep Learning Approach for NIDS". 9th EAI International Conference on Bio-inspired Information and Communications Technologies, At New Work.

[46] Yao h, Fu D, Zhang P, Li M, Liu Y. MSML: a novel multilevel semi-supervised machine learning framework for intrusion detection system. IEEE IoT J. 2018;6(2):1949-1959. https://doi.org/10.1109/JIOT.2018.2873125.

[47] Shen Y, Zheng K, Wu C, Zhang M, Niu X, Yang Y. An ensemble method based on selection using bat algorithm for intrusion detection. Comput J. 2018;61(4):526-538. https://doi.org/10.1093/comjnl/bxx101.

[48] Ali Mh, Al Mohammed BAD, Ismail A, Zolkipli MF. A new intrusion detection system based on fast learning network and particle swarm optimization. IEEE Access. 2018;6:20255-20261. https://doi.org/10.1109/ACCESS.2018.2820092.

[49] Jia Y, Wang M, Wang Y. Network intrusion detection algorithm based on deep neural network. IET Inf Secur. 2018;13(1):48-53. https:// doi.org/10.1049/iet-ifs.2018.5258.

[50] Wang Z. Deep learning-based intrusion detection with adversaries. IEEE Access. 2018;6:38367-38384. https://doi.org/10.1109/ACCESS. 2018.2854599.

[51] Yan B, han G. Effective feature extraction via stacked sparse autoencoder to improve intrusion detection system. IEEE Access. 2018;6:41238-41248. https://doi.org/10.1109/ACCESS.2018.2858277.

[52] Naseer S, Saleem Y, Khalid S, et al. Enhanced network anomaly detection based on deep neural networks. IEEE Access. 2018;6:48231-48246. https://doi.org/10.1109/ACCESS.2018.2863036.

[53] Xu C, Shen J, Du X, Zhang F. An intrusion detection system using a deep neural network with gated recurrent units. IEEE Access. 2018;6:48697-48707. https://doi.org/10.1109/ACCESS.2018.2867564.

[54] Al-Qatf M, Lasheng Y, Al-habib M, Al-Sabahi K. Deep learning approach combining sparse autoencoder with SVM for network intrusion detection. IEEE Access. 2018;6:52843-52856. https://doi.org/10.1109/ACCESS.2018.2869577.

[55] Marir N, Wang h, Feng G, Li B, Jia M. Distributed abnormal behavior detection approach based on deep belief network and ensemble svm using spark. IEEE Access. 2018;6:59657-59671. https://doi.org/10.1109/ACCESS.2018.2875045.

[56] Hamed Alqahtani, Iqbal H., Sarker Asra Kalim, Syed Md. Minhaz Hossain,Sheikh Ikhlaq, Sohrab Hossain "Cyber

Intrusion Detection Using Machine Learning Classification Techniques" International Conference on Computing Science, Communication and Security COMS2 2020.

[57] H. Al Najada, 'Cyber Intrusion Prediction and Taxonomy System Using Deep Learning And Distributed Big Data Processing', IEEE, pp. 631-638, 2018.

[58] A. Shenfielda, 'Intelligent intrusion detection systems using artificial neural networks', ICT Express 4, pp. 95-99, 2018.

[59] D. AKSU, 'Detecting Port Scan Attempts with Comparative Analysis of Deep Learning and Support Vector Machine Algorithms', IEEE, pp. 77-80, 2018.

[60] H. Liu, 'CNN and RNN based payload classification methods for attack', Knowledge-Based Systems, pp. 332-341, 2019.

[61] B. Roy, 'A Deep Learning Approach for Intrusion Detection in Internet of Things using Bi-Directional Long Short-Term Memory Recurrent Neural Network', IEEE, 2018.

[62] J. Yan, 'A Comparative Study of Off-Line Deep Learning Based Network Intrusion Detection', IEEE, pp. 299-305, 2018.

[63] A. Dawoud, 'Deep learning and software-defined networks: Towards secure IoT architecture', Internet of Things, pp. 82-89, 2018.

[64] M AL-Hawawreh, 'Identification of malicious activities in industrial internet of things based on deep learning models', Journal of Information Security and Applications, pp. 1-11, 2018.

[65] F. Feng, 'Anomaly detection in ad-hoc networks based on deep learning model: A plug and play device', Ad Hoc Networks, pp. 82- 89, 2019.

[66] Benamar Bouyeddou, Benamar Kadri, FouziHarrou, Ying Sun,DDOS-attacks detection using an efficient measurement-based statistical mechanism, Engineering Science and Technology, an International Journal, Volume 23, Issue 4, 2020, Pages 870-878, ISSN 2215-0986,

[67] Shone, N., Ngoc, T., Phai, V., and Shi, Q., 2018. A Deep Learning Approach to Network Intrusion Detection. IEEE Transactions on Emerging Topics in Computational Intelligence, 2(1), pp.41-50.

[68] W. Lin, H. Lin, P. Wang, B. Wu and J. Tsai, "Using convolutional neural networks to network intrusion detection for cyber threats," 2018 IEEE International Conference on Applied System Invention (ICASI), Chiba, 2018, pp. 1107-1110.

[69] S. Park, M. Kim and S. Lee, "Anomaly Detection for HTTP Using Convolutional Autoencoders," in IEEE Access, vol. 6, pp. 70884-70901, 2018, doi: 10.1109/ACCESS.2018.2881003.

[70] Ajith Abraham, Ravi Jain, Johnson Thomas, Sang Yong Han, D-SCIDS: Distributed soft computing intrusion detection system, Journal of Network and Computer Applications, Volume 30, Issue 1, 2007, Pages 81-98, ISSN 1084-8045

[71] C. Yin, 'A Deep Learning Approach for Intrusion Detection Using Recurrent Neural Networks', IEEE Access, cilt 5, pp. 21954-21962, 2017.

[72] Yin C, Zhu Y, Fei J, he X. A deep learning approach for intrusion detection using recurrent neural networks. IEEE Access. 2017;5:21954-21961. https://doi.org/10.1109/ACCESS.2017.2762418.

[73] A. Diro, 'Distributed attack detection scheme using deep learning approach for Internet of Things', Future Generation Computer Systems, pp. 761-768, 2017.

[74] Tahir Mehmood1 and Helmi B Md Rais2 "Machine Learning Algorithms in Context of Intrusion Detection" 3rd International Conference on Computer and Information Sciences (ICCOINS),2016.

[75] Y. Liu, 'Intrusion detection based on IDBM', IEEE, pp. 173-178, 2016. T. Tang, 'Deep Learning Approach for Network Intrusion Detection in Software Defined Networking', IEEE, pp. 1-7, 2016

[76] J. Jabez, B. Muthukumar,Intrusion Detection System (IDS): Anomaly Detection Using Outlier Detection Approach,Procedia Computer Science, Volume 48, 2015, Pages 338-346,ISSN 1877-0509.

[77] Adel Sabry Eesa, Z. O. A novel feature-selection approach based on the cuttlefish optimization algorithm for intrusion detection systems. Expert Systems with Applications,ELSEVIER 2014.

[78] A.M.Chandrashekhar, K. . Fortification of hybrid intrusion detection system using variants of neural networks support vector machines. International Journal of Network Security Its Applications (IJNSA) 2013.

[79] Gisung Kim, S. L. A novel hybrid intrusion detection method integrating anomaly detection with misuse detection. Expert Systems with Applications,ELSEVIER 2013.

[80] Bose, A. A. (2012). The combined approach for anomaly detection using neural networks clustering techniques. Computer Science Engineering: An International Journal (CSEIJ) 2012.

[81] Levent Koc, T. A network intrusion detection system based on a Hidden Na¨ıve Bayes multiclass classifier. Expert Systems with Applications,ELSEVIER 2012.

[82] Muna Mhammad T. Jawhar, M. M. Design Network Intrusion Detection System using hybrid. International Journal of Computer Science and Security 2010.

[83] Min Seok Mok, S. Y. Random effects logistic regression model for anomaly detection. Expert Systems with Applications,ELSEVIER, 2010

[84] X. Gao, C. Shan, C. Hu, Z. Niu and Z. Liu, ”An Adaptive Ensemble Machine Learning Model for Intrusion Detection,” in IEEE Access, vol. 7, pp. 82512-82521, 2019, doi: 10.1109/ACCESS.2019.2923640.

[85] M. Bahrololum, E. S. Anomaly based Intrusion Detection System, International Journal of Computer Networks Communications (IJCNC),2009.

[86] K. Hwang, M. Cai, Y. Chen and M. Qin, ”Hybrid Intrusion Detection with Weighted Signature Generation over Anomalous Internet Episodes,” in IEEE Transactions on Dependable and Secure Computing, vol. 4, no. 1, pp. 41-55, Jan.-March 2007.

[87] K. Ilgun, ”USTAT: a real-time intrusion detection system for UNIX,” Proceedings 1993 IEEE Computer Society Symposium on Research in Security and Privacy, 1993, pp. 16-28, doi: 10.1109/RISP.1993.287646

[88] J. Liu, W. Zhang, Z. Tang, Y. Xie, T. Ma, J. Zhang, G. Zhang, and J. P. Niyoyita, ”Adaptive intrusion detection via GA-GOGMM-based pattern learning with fuzzy rough set-based attribute selection,” Expert Systems with Applications, vol. 139, p. 112845, 2020

[89] M. Almseidin and S. Kovacs, ”Intrusion detection mechanism using fuzzy rule interpolation,” arXiv preprint arXiv:1904.08790, 2019.

[90] P. Boonyopakorn, ”The Optimization and Enhancement of Network Intrusion Detection through Fuzzy Association Rules,” in 2019 6th International Conference on Technical Education (ICTechEd6), 2019, pp. 1-5

[91] Mutep Y Al Yousef, Nabih T Abdelmajeed, Dynamically Detecting Security Threats and Updating a Signature-Based Intrusion Detection System’s Database, Procedia Computer Science, Volume 159, 2019,Pages 1507-1516,ISSN 1877-0509, https://doi.org/10.1016/j.procs.2019.09.321

[92] H. Almutairi and N. T. Abdelmajeed, "Innovative signature based intrusion detection system: Parallel processing and minimized database," 2017 International Conference on the Frontiers and Advances in Data Science (FADS), Xi'an, China, 2017, pp. 114-119, doi: 10.1109/FADS.2017.8253208.

[93] A. F. A. Pinem and E. B. Setiawan, "Implementation of classification and regression Tree (CART) and fuzzy logic algorithm for intrusion detection system," in Information and Communication Technology (ICoICT), 2015 3rd International Conference on, 2015, pp. 266- 271.

[94] W. Yassin, N. I. Udzir, A. Abdullah, M. T. Abdullah, H. Zulzalil and Z. Muda, "Signature- Based Anomaly intrusion detection using Integrated data mining classifiers," 2014 Inter- national Symposium on Biometrics and Security Technologies (ISBAST), Kuala Lumpur, Malaysia, 2014, pp. 232-237, doi: 10.1109/ISBAST.2014.7013127..

[95] S. Benferhat, A. Boudjelida, K. Tabia, H. Drias, An intrusion detection and alert correlation approach based on revising probabilistic classifiers using expert knowledge, Int. J. Appl. Intell. 38 (4) (2013) 520–540

[96] Phuong Do, Ho-Seok Kang, and Sung-Ryul Kim. 2013. Improved signature based intrusion detection using clustering rule for decision tree. In Proceedings of the 2013 Research in Adaptive and Convergent Systems (RACS '13). Association for Computing Machinery, New York, NY, USA, 347–348.

[97] H.T. Elshoush, I.M. Osman, An improved framework for intrusion alert correlation, in: WCE'12:Proceedings of the 2012 World Congress on Engineering, 2012, pp. 1–6

[98] S. Mabu, C. Chen, N. Lu, K. Shimada, and K. Hirasawa, "An intrusion-detection model based on fuzzy class-association-rule mining using genetic network programming," IEEE Transactions on Systems, Man, and Cybernetics, Part C (Applications and Reviews), vol. 41, pp. 130-139, 2011.

[99] R. Sadoddin, A.A. Ghorbani, An incremental frequent structure mining framework for real-time alert correlation, Comp. Sec. 28 (2009) 153–173.

[100] S.O. Al-Mamory, H. Zhang, Ids alerts correlation using grammar-based approach, J. Comp. Virol. 28 (3) (2009) 271–282

[101] M. Soleimani, A.A. Ghorbani, Critical episode mining in intrusion detection alerts, in: Proceedings of the Communication

Networks and Services Research Conference, IEEE Computer Society, 2008, pp. 157–164.

[102] C. Thomas, N. Balakrishnan, Performance enhancement of intrusion detection systems using advances in sensor fusion, in: Fusion'08: Proceedings of the 11th International Conference on Information Fusion, 2008, pp. 1671–1677.

[103] F. Massicotte, M. Couture, Y. Labiche, Model-driven, network-context sensitive intrusion detection, in: MoDELS '07: Proceedings of the 10th International Conference on Model Driven Engineering Languages and Systems, Lecture Notes in Computer Science, 2007, pp. 61–75.

[104] F. Maggi, S. Zanero, On the use of different statistical tests for alert correlation: short paper, in: Proceedings of the 10th International Conference on Recent Advances in Intrusion Detection, RAID'07, SpringerVerlag, pp. 167–177.

[105] D. Brumley, J. Newso, D. Song, H. Wang, S. Jha, Towards automatic generation of vulnerability-based signatures, in: SP '06: Proceedings of the 2006 IEEE Symposium on Security and Privacy, IEEE Computer Society, 2006, pp. 2–16.

[106] T. Pietraszek, A. Tanner, Data mining and machine learning – towards reducing false positives in intrusion detection, Inform. Sec. Tech. Rep. 10 (3) (2005) 169–18

[107] D. Yu, D. Frincke, A novel framework for alert correlation and understanding, in: ACNS '04: Proceedings of the 2004 International Conference on Applied Cryptoraphy and Network Security, Lecture Notes in Computer Science, 2004, pp. 452–466

[108] Kruegel C., Toth T. Using Decision Trees to Improve Signature-Based Intrusion De- tection. In: Vigna G., Kruegel C., Jonsson E. (eds) Recent Advances in Intrusion Detection. RAID 2003. Lecture Notes in Computer Science, vol 2820. Springer, Berlin, Heidelberg 2003.

[109] R. Sommer, V. Paxson, Enhancing byte-level network intrusion detection signatures with context, in: CCS '03: Proceedings of the 10th ACM Conference on Computer and Communications Security, ACM, 2003, pp. 262–271.

[110] G. Vigna, W. Robertson, V. Kher, R.A. Kemmerer, A stateful intrusion detection system for world-wide web servers, in: ACSAC '03: Proceedings of the 19th Annual Computer Security Applications Conference, IEEE Computer Society, 2003, p. 34.

[111] P. Ning, Y. Cui, S.D. Reeves, D. Xu, Towards automating intrusion alert analysis, in: 2003 Workshop on Statistical and Machine Learning Techniques in Computer Intrusion Detection, 2003, pp. 1–19.

[112] S. Cheung, U. Lindqvist, M.W. Fong, Modeling multistep cyber attacks for scenario recognition, in: DISCEX '03: Proceedings of the 3rd International DARPA Information Survivability Conferenc Intrusion Detection System : A survey", International Journal of Emerging Technologies and Innovative Research (www.jetir.org — UGC and issn Approved), ISSN:2349-5162, Vol.6, Issue 6, page no. pp440-446, June-2019e and Exposition, IEEE, 2003, pp. 284–292.

[113] C. Kruegel, F. Valeur, G. Vigna, R.A. Kemmerer, Stateful intrusion detection for high-speed networks, in: SP '02: Proceedings of the 2002 IEEE Symposium on Security and Privacy, IEEE Computer Society, 2002, pp. 285–294.

[114] F. Cuppens, F. Autrel, A. Miege, S. Benferhat, R.M. Ege, Correlation in an intrusion detection process, in: SECI '02: Proceedings of the 2002 International Conference on Security of Communications on the Internet, INRIA, 2002, pp. 153–183.

[115] K. Julisch, M. Dacier, Mining intrusion detection alarms for actionable knowledge, in: SIGKDD '02: Proceedings of the 8th ACM SIGKDD International Conference on Knowledge Discovery and Data Mining, ACM, 2002, pp. 366–375.

[116] S. Krishnamurthy, A. Sen, Stateful intrusion detection system (sids), in: ICIW '01: Proceedings of the 2nd IEE Conference on Information Warfare and Security, IEEE, 2001, pp. 1–10.

[117] Ansam Khraisat, Iqbal Gondal, Peter Vamplew, Joarder Kamruzzaman and Ammar Alazab, "Hybrid Intrusion Detection System Based on the Stacking Ensemble of C5 De- cision Tree Classifier and One Class Support Vector Machine" MDPI Electronics 2020, 9, 173; doi:10.3390/electronics9010173

[118] R. Kumar and D. Sharma, "Signature-Anomaly Based Intrusion Detection Algorithm," 2018 Second International Conference on Electronics, Communication and Aerospace Tech- nology (ICECA), Coimbatore, 2018, pp. 836-841.

[119] S. M. Hussein, "Performance Evaluation of Intrusion Detection System Using Anomaly and Signature Based Algorithms to Reduction False Alarm Rate and Detect Unknown Attacks," 2016 International Conference on Computational Science and

Computational Intelligence (CSCI), Las Vegas, NV, 2016, pp. 1064-1069.

[120] A. S. Desai and D. P. Gaikwad, "Real time hybrid intrusion detection system using signa- ture matching algorithm and fuzzy-GA," 2016 IEEE International Conference on Advances in Electronics, Communication and Computer Technology (ICAECCT), Pune, 2016, pp. 291-294. doi: 10.1109/ ICAECCT.2016.7942601

[121] M. Ali Aydın, A. Halim Zaim, K. G¨okhan Ceylan, A hybrid intrusion detection system design for computer network security, Computers Electrical Engineering, Volume 35, Issue 3, 2009, Pages 517-526, ISSN 0045-7906, https://doi.org/10.1016/j. compeleceng.200

[122] K. Hwang, M. Cai, Y. Chen and M. Qin, "Hybrid Intrusion Detection with Weighted Signa- ture Generation over Anomalous Internet Episodes," in IEEE Transactions on Dependable and Secure Computing, vol. 4, no. 1, pp. 41-55, Jan.-March 2007.

[123] Hussain, S. G. Abbas, M. Husnain, U. U. Fayyaz, F. Shahzad and G. A. Shah, "IoT DoS and DDoS Attack Detection using ResNet" 2020 IEEE 23rd International Multitopic Conference (INMIC), Bahawalpur, Pakistan, 2020, pp. 1-6, doi: 10.1109/ INMIC50486.2020.9318216.

Made in the USA
Monee, IL
12 November 2026

39e3ee7d-ce1b-4433-be9f-75a819b878a1R01